This book belongs to:

THE

Little Women

COOKBOOK

Novel Takes on Classic Recipes
from Meg, Jo, Beth, Amy, and Friends

Jenne Bergstrom
- AND -
Miko Osada

ULYSSES PRESS

Published in the United States by:
ULYSSES PRESS
P.O. Box 3440
Berkeley, CA 94703
www.ulyssespress.com

ISBN: 978-1-61243-943-3
Library of Congress Control Number: 2019942070

Little Women illustrations and quotes are from the 1896 edition published by Little, Brown, and Company written by Louisa May Alcott with illustrations by Frank T. Merrill and Edmund H. Garrett.

Printed in China by Sunny Print Co. LTD through Four Colour Print Group

10 9 8 7 6 5 4 3 2 1

Acquisitions editor: Casie Vogel
Managing editor: Claire Chun
Editor: Lauren Harrison
Proofreader: Kate St. Clair
Front cover and interior design: Malea Clark-Nicholson
Little Women illustrations from scans by the Internet Archive courtesy of the New York Public Library:
    pages 3, 4, 6, 12, 13, 16, 18, 26, 27, 30, 31, 38, 40, 41, 46, 50, 54, 64, 66, 67, 68, 72, 73, 80, 81, 82, 86, 98, 101, 111, 112, 113, 116, 117, 118, 124, 127, 132, 133, 134, 146, 152, 160, 166, 173, 175
Artwork from shutterstock.com: silhouettes © fresher; food and equipment icons © Kraphi and © Ku_suriuri; line ornaments © Roberto Castillo
Photographs from shutterstock.com: omelet © Evgeniya863; white cake © Malivan_Iuliia; lemonade and lemon water © Africa Studio; roast beef © Lisovskaya Natalia; catsup © Vania Georgieva; peach pie © Tammy Venezia; seeded muffins © SMarina; sweet potatoes © MShev; apple jelly © picturepartners; roast chicken © Koliadzynska Iryna; raspberry ice cream © pearl7; French chocolate © Elena Pyatkova; charlotte rosse © Nigina Sharipova; pink ice cream © Stephanie Frey; potato rolls © cesarz; pickled eggs © Olga Markova; cale-cannon © Monkey Business Images; coffee © Sunny Forest; English muffins © Stephen Gibson; biscuits © Brenda Carson; tea © SedovaY

This book is dedicated to our parents,
who raised us to be readers and eaters.

Contents

PREFACE

If you've picked up this book, we're guessing that you've probably already read *Little Women*, or at least watched one of the many movie and TV adaptations. But in case you're a more casual visitor, here's a quick recap: The story follows four sisters, Meg, Jo, Beth, and Amy, who live in New England during the American Civil War era. Their father is away as a chaplain in the Union Army and their finances are not in great shape, but they do their best to enjoy life and improve themselves despite difficult times. Over the 10 years that the book covers, they grow from idealistic teenagers to mature adult women (with one sad exception). Even though many details of daily life have changed, the characters are so lovable and realistic that *Little Women* has been in print continuously for over 150 years! We both read our copies to pieces as children and teens, and we continue to find new things to enjoy in the story as adults.

We, the authors of this cookbook, are librarians by day and spend our free time making food and beverages from our favorite stories. Re-creating fictitious dishes is an immersive, 4D experience of our most beloved books. Especially in *Little Women*, where the novel centers on domestic life, the menus the characters choose and enjoy give us hints and insights about their personalities and priorities, and help us better understand them. Having a themed meal makes it that much easier to pretend we're in that era—we think of the food as an extra detail to cosplay! And so we asked the question: What exactly would the March sisters have eaten? After perusing hundreds of 19th-century recipes (or receipts, as they called them back then), we present you this book as our response to this worthy query.

A BITE-SIZED HISTORY

Let's start with a little history of Northern Civil War–era cuisine. New Englanders, as descendants of Puritans, liked meals of baked or stewed meat, boiled vegetables, and pie.[1] But you're mistaken if you assume their food was all boring and bland. For one thing, Victorians made a vast array of their own condiments to season their food—curries, catsups, pickles, and gravies of all kinds. (We've included just a few samples in this book for you to try.) Plus, international cuisine already had a strong presence on the middle-class table in the 19th century. In the mid-1800s, advances in the railroad and canning industries allowed supplies to be sent quickly from one end of the country to the other, and even the most budget-conscious cookbooks required ingredients that had to be imported from all over the world: chocolate, coffee, tea, spices, citrus fruits, and tapioca, for example.[2]

FOOD IS TRENDY

Going through old cookbooks makes you realize that food is as trendy as fashion. Dishes, ingredients, and culinary methods that were

1   Helen Zoe Veit, *Food in the Civil War Era: The North* (East Lansing: Michigan State University Press, 2014), 14.
2   Veit, *Food in the Civil War Era: The North*, 31–32.

popular in the 1800s might surprise or weird us out today, just as the idea of wearing a hoopskirt daily is decidedly unappealing to most modern readers. For example, we prefer to eat vegetables *al dente*, so to us, it seems like Victorians cooked theirs for a ridiculously long time. (They want us to boil the summer squash for 45 minutes!?) More differences between Americans then and now: Victorian bakers were reaching for their nutmeg where we would add vanilla, and nutmeg was also as common in savory dishes as pepper. We struggled to find a cookie recipe from the period, but there were endless options for blanc-manges and puddings. Finally, there are whole genres of cooking that aren't included in the typical American repertoire anymore. "Sweetmeats," for example, included preserved and candied fruits. And in most 19th-century cookbooks, there's a chapter devoted to "invalid cookery," or food for the sick, since medical care was usually administered at home.[3] (See Dainty Dishes starting on page 72 for more details!)

COOKING WAS A CHORE

Even for the most enthusiastic 21st-century chef, cooking can still feel like a chore sometimes. But imagine if you lived in the 1800s, when the whole process was a gigantic pain. First, you'd have to get the ingredients ready.... Wait, but there was no one-stop grocery store, so shopping meant visiting multiple shops. Food was only available according to season: fresh produce in summer and early autumn, shellfish in winter, and lamb in spring. (Take a look at *What Shall We Eat? A Manual for Housekeepers*, an 1868 cookbook that

suggests menus for every day of the year. It's fascinating!) Chicken is a standard dinner meat now, but back then, poultry was considered fancy because you had to take the extra step of plucking the feathers—you might have even bought it live from the butcher, so you'd have to kill it first. You would also have to tend to the home garden and livestock, if you had any.

And you're still not ready to begin cooking. You'd have to pump and haul water, carry coal, chop wood, and start and watch the fire. This last task was no small feat. Ovens had no handy thermometers or switches, so you had to know how to control the temperature by building the fire a certain way. That's why old recipes don't say, "Bake for 45 minutes at 350°F." Instead, their instructions are more like, "Bake in a quick oven till done." Helpful, right? Victorian cookbooks assume readers have a lot of prior knowledge, and they often don't list specific ingredient amounts either. That's why their directions can read like the Technical Challenge on *The Great British Baking Show*.

NOVEL TAKES ON CLASSIC RECIPES

The technical challenge of making a historical receipt (recipe) is fun, but can often be frustrating if you're not an experienced cook. In this book, we've tried as much as possible to keep to the flavors and textures of the actual food from the era, so that you can literally get a taste of what it was like to live 150 years ago. For the most part, we've been pleasantly surprised at how good Victorian food is—there's a perception that it's all flavorless boiled things, but these simple

---

3   Veit, *Food in the Civil War Era*, 24.

preparations really let the ingredients shine. Time after time we would read a recipe from an old cookbook and think that there was no possible way it would work, only to be shocked at how delicious it turned out to be.

We've made some modifications to ingredients where they're no longer readily available in the U.S. (mutton, dried currants) or now known to be toxic (bitter almond) or prohibitively expensive (recipes containing truffles, or 100 oysters, were left out). We've also updated techniques since most people no longer have a smokehouse, a cooking fireplace with a roasting spit, or a special muslin bag for the purpose of boiling squash—not to mention an army of apprentice cooks to make French sauces, or a kitchen maid to whip egg whites by hand.

We've sprinkled a few original 19th-century receipts through this book so you can compare our modern versions, side by side. The main difference between our recipes and their historical counterparts is that we've tested ours, given specific measurements and clear instructions, and done our best to take out the guesswork so you can just go ahead and cook!

Note: Unless otherwise specified, we tested these recipes using:

- Salted butter (we believe in salted butter for almost everything!)
- Diamond Crystal kosher salt (the large crystals are less salty by volume than regular table salt, so use less if your salt is fine-grained)
- Unrefined cane sugar (rather than pure white, it's a golden color, with a slight molasses flavor—tastier and more historically accurate, but regular white sugar is fine with no adjustments)

- All-purpose flour (flour production was a whole different thing back then, so we just went with what's easy to get)
- Large eggs (eggs were most likely smaller in the 1900s, but we've adjusted since small eggs are harder to find these days)

WHO IS MRS. CORNELIUS?

We consulted a wide variety of historical cookbooks in compiling these recipes (see page 174 for a full list), but one in particular stands out: *The Young Housekeeper's Friend*, first published in 1846. It is actually mentioned by name more than once in *Little Women*, so it became our first point of reference for the dishes in this book. And the author, Mary Hooker Cornelius, was from Andover, Massachusetts—not far from Concord, where Louisa May Alcott's family lived.

In the preface Mrs. Cornelius writes, "I have seen many a young lady, just entered upon the duties of married life, perplexed and prematurely care-worn, for want of experience, or a little good instruction, in regard to the simplest domestic processes; and often have felt, with the sincerest sympathy, an earnest wish to render her some effectual aid."

Her wish seems to have come true: The cookbook was quite popular in its day, and went through several editions—with good reason, as we discovered. Of all the cookbooks we used in our research, the receipts in this one were always the tastiest and most reliable!

As you go through our recipes, you'll see the occasional tip marked "Friendly Advice"—these are hints from us in the spirit of Mrs. Cornelius, to make your cooking easier, avoid disasters, or suggest alternative ways to serve a dish.

Which March Sister Are You?

Before we embark on our culinary journey, let's see if you're a Meg, Jo, Beth, or Amy. Take this personality quiz to find out! Here's what you do:

STEP 1: For each numbered statement, decide if you agree or disagree. Circle the letters in the column for your response.

STEP 2: Count the number of As that were circled and note it on the next page. Do the same for the Bs, Cs, and Ds.

STEP 3: Take a look on the next page to see which sister you are!

	AGREE	DISAGREE
1. I consider myself a creative person.	B D	A C
2. I like big social gatherings.	A B D	C
3. I've often dreamed of falling in love.	A	B C D
4. I love puttering around the house.	A C	B D
5. I seek adventure in my life.	B D	A C
6. I can't keep track of my stuff—I lose and break things all the time.	B	A C D
7. I admit I have a temper.	B D	A C
8. If I could choose, I'd live in a gorgeous mansion over a cute cottage.	A D	B C
9. I kind of enjoy shocking people.	B	A C D
10. I want to earn acclaim for my work.	B D	A C
11. Flirting is fun for me.	A D	B C
12. I'm always coming up with ideas.	B D	A C
13. I make friends easily.	A B D	C
14. My clothes are very important to me.	A D	B C
15. It's hard for me to say I'm sorry.	B D	A C

Number of As: _____   Number of Bs: _____   Number of Cs: _____   Number of Ds: _____

Each letter represents a March sister. Which letter do you have the most of?

Mostly As

You are most like ... Meg!

Meg is sweet, patient, and domestic. These are characteristics she shares with Beth, but Meg is more social, flirtatious, and romantic. She appreciates nice things and little luxuries, especially clothes. Cook up a delicious dinner with Meg in Chapter 1 (page 12).

Mostly Bs

You are most like ... Jo!

Jo seeks adventure and dreams of accomplishing great things. A conventional life is not for Jo. She has a temper and can be heedless. Jo is a social creature and likes being around people (although she has a distaste for fancy company and occasions). Take a bite out of life with Jo's favorite foods in Chapter 2 (page 40).

Mostly Cs

You are most like ... Beth!

Beth is kind, careful, and considerate. She prefers to stay in a small circle of trusted loved ones than to go out among strangers. She likes being at home more than anywhere else. Enjoy a night in with Beth's cozy dishes and Victorian remedies in Chapter 3 (page 66).

Mostly Ds

You are most like ... Amy!

Like Jo, Amy is creative and adventurous, and she dreams of achieving greatness. Amy can be temperamental and has a weakness for pretty things. Popular and gifted with social grace, Amy enjoys parties, where she can be the belle of the ball. Indulge your inner Amy with treats in Chapter 4 (page 80).

If you take a look, the sisters have different traits they share with each of the others. Jo and Amy are often presented as opposites, so aren't you surprised, going through the questions, just how much they have in common? If Jo and Amy butt heads, it's not necessarily because they're too different!

Even if you get a perfect 15-point match on this quiz, none of us is a complete clone of any one March girl. The beauty of both the book's characters and ourselves is that we are multifaceted beings, and that means readers can find something to relate to in each of the four sisters.

CHAPTER 1

Meg

In spite of her small vanities, Margaret had a sweet and pious nature, which unconsciously influenced her sisters, especially Jo, who loved her very tenderly, and obeyed her because her advice was so gently given.

CHAPTER 2: "A MERRY CHRISTMAS"

Genteel, sentimental Meg longs for romance, beauty, and comfort. She loves parties, amateur theater, dressing up in fancy outfits, and adding pretty touches to make things nicer. As the oldest sister, she can still remember when their family had money, so she has the hardest time with their relative poverty. She can't afford new clothes, but she does her best to remake her old ones to suit the new fashion ... with mixed results. Eventually, she comes to realize that simplicity and good taste suit her best, and can be achieved even with her limited resources.

Despite her dreams of luxury, Meg defies even her own expectations by choosing love over money, and elects to be a poor man's wife. When she sets up her own household, she's willing to move into a small cottage and live a modest lifestyle in order to be with her beloved John Brooke, but she has high standards for herself as a housekeeper. She resolves that her home will always be perfectly clean and ready for unexpected company, with her as the perfect hostess in a pretty dress. (You can see where this is going—there's definitely going to be a day when her husband brings home a friend for dinner to find Meg sobbing into her apron, the kitchen a disaster, and the house in total disarray.)

Meg likes cooking, although she needs practice before she gets the hang of it. Young Meg proudly sends Laurie blanc-mange (page 114), her best dish, when he's sick, and tries to make an omelet for her mother (who very kindly does not tell her how badly it turned out). As a newly married woman, Meg is determined to master the culinary arts by working through every recipe in *The Young Housekeeper's Friend* book, and despite some embarrassing set-backs, she eventually does become a competent cook and homemaker, the kind of person friends and neighbors come to for advice and encouragement with their own domestic difficulties. She truly enjoys making her home a pleasant and beautiful place, with a happy family around her.

A modern Meg is the one who can throw a real dinner party, with hors d'oeuvres and cloth napkins. Her house is full of amazing vintage yard sale finds, and her kitchen is spotless when anyone comes over. If you're a close friend (or sister), you realize all these accomplishments don't always come easily—Meg is the queen of the Pinterest fail, but unlike Jo, she would never send photos of her latest hilarious disaster. Instead, Meg would toil in secret until she's able to produce a beautiful success.

In this chapter, you'll find Meg's triumphs (the ice cream she makes for Beth, her "remarkably plummy" wedding-cake), her failures (the omelet that Marmee threw away, the currant jelly that wouldn't jell), and a selection of simple weekday recipes, based on the classics that good Mrs. Cornelius wrote for the young housekeepers of the mid-1800s.

Omelet for Mother

There was plenty of food in the larder, and, while Beth and Amy set the table, Meg and Jo got breakfast, wondering, as they did so, why servants ever talked about hard work.

"I shall take some up to mother, though she said we were not to think of her, for she'd take care of herself," said Meg, who presided, and felt quite matronly behind the teapot.

So a tray was fitted out before anyone began, and taken up, with the cook's compliments. The boiled tea was very bitter, the omelet scorched, and the biscuits speckled with saleratus; but Mrs. March received her repast with thanks and laughed heartily over it after Jo was gone.

"Poor little souls, they will have a hard time, I'm afraid; but they won't suffer, and it will do them good," she said, producing the more palatable viands with which she had provided herself, and disposing of the bad breakfast, so that their feelings might not be hurt, —a motherly little deception, for which they were grateful.

CHAPTER II: "EXPERIMENTS"

Everyone has to start somewhere, and this is clearly Meg's first attempt at making breakfast. Never cook an omelet on high heat, or you'll end up with a scorched one like hers! It may sound strange to put nutmeg in a savory egg dish, but it adds a nice flavor, almost like a different sort of pepper. Serve the omelet with biscuits (page 162) and tea (page 172).

Makes 1 serving

- 2 eggs
- 2 tablespoons milk
- 1 tablespoon minced parsley
- 1 tablespoon minced onion
- ½ teaspoon freshly grated nutmeg
- pinch of salt
- ½ tablespoon butter, or as needed for frying

1. In a small bowl, beat the eggs and milk together with a fork until a bit frothy.

2. Add the parsley, onion, nutmeg, and salt and mix well.

3. Heat a small frying pan over medium heat and melt the butter in it. Make sure the butter coats the whole pan and goes up the sides a bit.

4. Pour in the egg mixture and put a lid on the pan. Let cook for 1 to 2 minutes, until the eggs are set around the edges but still a little loose in the middle.

5. Use a wide spatula to fold the omelet in half (it should be a little browned on the outside) and slide it onto a plate to serve.

Friendly Advice: Garnish with a little extra parsley and the cook's compliments.

Meg

Ice Cream Made by Lovely Peg

THE JUNGFRAU TO BETH

God bless you, dear Queen Bess!
May nothing you dismay,
But health and peace and happiness
Be yours, this Christmas day.

Here's fruit to feed our busy bee,
And flowers for her nose;
Here's music for her pianee,
An Afghan for her toes.

A portrait of Joanna, see,
By Raphael No. 2,
Who laboured with great industry
To make it fair and true.

Accept a ribbon red, I beg,
For Madam Purrer's tail;
And ice cream made by lovely Peg,—
A Mont Blanc in a pail.

Their dearest love my makers laid
Within my breast of snow:
Accept it, and the Alpine maid,
From Laurie and from Jo.

CHAPTER 22: "PLEASANT MEADOWS"

This method uses all milk and no cream, but adds egg yolks—a better option for an invalid with a delicate stomach. It's a bit less rich but still tastes creamy.

Makes 4 servings

- 2 egg yolks
- ⅓ cup sugar
- 1 tablespoon vanilla extract
- pinch of salt
- 2 cups milk

1. Stir together the egg yolks, sugar, vanilla, and salt in a small bowl.

2. Heat the milk in a medium saucepan over medium heat until it is just barely bubbling at the edges, then turn the heat off.

3. Add a few spoonfuls of the hot milk to the egg mixture and stir well.

4. Add the egg mixture to the pan of milk slowly, stirring constantly.

5. Return the pan to low heat and simmer, stirring constantly and scraping the bottom, until the mixture has thickened a bit, enough to coat the spoon. This should take 5 to 10 minutes—be patient! (If it gets too hot, it may curdle a bit, but don't worry; just run it through a fine strainer before you refrigerate it.)

6. Remove from the heat and transfer to a lidded container. Refrigerate overnight or until completely cold.

7. Freeze in an ice cream maker (hand-crank for authenticity, or electric for convenience), then serve immediately in cold bowls. If you store it in the freezer (it will keep well for several weeks), let it soften before serving since it can be a bit icy.

Friendly Advice: Alternatively, you can flavor the ice cream with a tablespoon of lemon juice and a teaspoon of lemon zest instead of the vanilla.

Meg

Meg and John's Plentiful Wedding Lunch

It wasn't at all the thing, I'm afraid, but the minute she was fairly married, Meg cried, "The first kiss for Marmee!" and, turning, gave it with her heart on her lips. During the next fifteen minutes she looked more like a rose than ever, for everyone availed themselves of their privileges to the fullest extent, from Mr. Laurence to old Hannah, who, adorned with a head-dress fearfully and wonderfully made, fell upon her in the hall, crying, with a sob and a chuckle, "Bless you, deary, a hundred times! The cake ain't hurt a mite, and everything looks lovely."

Everybody cleared up after that, and said something brilliant, or tried to, which did just as well, for laughter is ready when hearts are light. There was no display of gifts, for they were already in the little house, nor was there an elaborate breakfast, but a plentiful lunch of cake and fruit, dressed with flowers.

CHAPTER 25: "THE FIRST WEDDING"

Ah, we do love a good wedding. It's hard to put a finger on what exactly makes a nuptial event fun, but as it turns out, Meg and John's celebration has that X factor. And not because it's fancy! John isn't a rich man, and the party is very DIY: Meg makes her own dress; her sisters braid her hair; and John is still putting up the decorative garlands when the guests are arriving. Maybe it's precisely because of these personal touches that the ceremony is so charming. The whole scene overflows with love and fun, not only because of the romance between the couple, but also the sincere affection the guests have for each other and the bride and groom. Once the vows conclude with a round of kisses, everyone sits down to lots of cake and fruit, with a choice of water, lemonade, and coffee (page 140) to drink. The festivities culminate in a spontaneous dance in the garden around the newlyweds, with even crabby Aunt March joining in. Meg's stylish friend Sallie is charmed and declares the wedding the prettiest in an age.

Remarkably Plummy Wedding-Cake

"You may thank Hannah for saving your wedding-cake from destruction. I saw it going into your house as I came by, and if she hadn't defended it manfully I'd have had a pick at it, for it looked like a remarkably plummy one."

CHAPTER 24: "GOSSIP"

Well into the 20th century, a wedding-cake was traditionally a fruitcake, full of "plums" (raisins) and other dried fruits. This is still common in the UK; for example, at William and Kate's royal wedding in 2011, they had an eight-tier fruitcake! The Marches might have been strict enough about temperance to leave out the wine and brandy, especially considering that Meg is so anti-alcohol that she makes Laurie swear to give it up forever at her wedding, but Hannah might have slipped it in for the occasion. (And it sure does make it taste better. In fact, if you like a boozier cake, feel free to add extra.)

Warning: This recipe will give your mixer a workout! For the fruit, we used a mix of dark and golden raisins, and chopped prunes instead of currants. True dried currants are very difficult to find in the U.S., for boring historical reasons.

Makes 8 to 32 servings, depending how much your guests like fruitcake

For the cake:

- 1½ pounds raisins
- 1½ pounds chopped prunes
- ¼ pound candied citron
- 2 tablespoons fortified wine, like Malaga, Marsala, or sherry
- 2 tablespoons brandy
- ½ pound (2 sticks) butter, at room temperature, plus extra for the pan
- ½ pound (1 cup) sugar
- 5 eggs, at room temperature
- ¼ cup molasses
- ½ pound (2¼ cups) flour
- 1 teaspoon freshly grated nutmeg
- 1 teaspoon ground mace
- ½ teaspoon ground cloves

For the frosting:

- 1 teaspoon cornstarch
- 3 egg whites
- 1 pound (2⅓ cups) superfine baking sugar
- juice of ½ lemon (about 1 tablespoon)

PREPARE THE CAKE:

1. In a very large bowl, combine the raisins, prunes, and citron with the wine and brandy and set aside. Periodically give it a stir.

2. Butter a 9-inch springform pan.

3. Cream the butter in the bowl of a stand mixer on high speed using the paddle attachment, until light and fluffy, about 3 minutes.

4. Add the sugar, and beat for 5 minutes, scraping down the sides periodically.

5. Add the eggs, one at a time, and beat on high speed until each one is thoroughly incorporated.

6. Add the molasses. Beat for 10 minutes and then scrape down the sides. Repeat twice, for a total of 30 minutes of beating. (Just be glad you don't have to do it by hand for "at least two hours," like it says in the original recipe!)

7. While the batter is mixing, sift the flour, nutmeg, mace, and cloves together twice so you have them ready to add. If you let the batter sit without beating, it will quickly lose its fluffiness.

8. At the last 10 minutes of beating, preheat the oven to 300°F.

9. Add the flour mixture in three parts to the batter and mix on slow speed until just combined.

10. Add the batter to the bowl with the dried fruit and mix well. Transfer to the prepared pan—it should be about three-quarters full.

11. Bake for about 75 minutes, or until a toothpick inserted in the center comes out mostly clean.

12. Remove the cake from the pan and let it cool on a rack while you make the frosting. It's okay if the cake's still warm when you frost it.

Friendly Advice: If the eggs are cold, the batter will curdle! You can warm them in a bowl of hot water if you forgot to take them out ahead of time.

PREPARE THE FROSTING:

1. In the bowl of a stand mixer using the whisk attachment on high speed, combine the cornstarch with the egg whites and beat to stiff peaks.

2. Add the sugar, a little at a time, while beating at medium speed. Scrape down the sides often.

3. Once all the sugar is added, switch to high speed and beat for 15 minutes, stopping occasionally to scrape down the sides.

4. Preheat the oven to 250°F.

5. Add the lemon juice and beat another 5 minutes. The frosting will be pure white and rather stiff.

6. Spread the frosting all over the cake in pretty swirls. Place the cake in the oven for 15 minutes to let the frosting harden. If the weather is dry, you can also just leave it out on the counter for several hours or overnight.

Friendly Advice: Before frosting, put your cake on whatever dish (not plastic) you want to serve it from, because if you try to move it later, the frosting will crack.

Get the Receipt

Our cake is a very scaled-down version of the one Meg and John would've had. Here's the recipe from *The Young Housekeeper's Friend*:

Five pounds each of flour, butter, and sugar, six of raisins, twelve of currants, two of citron, fifty eggs, half a pint of good Malaga wine, three ounces of nutmegs, three of cinnamon, one and a half of mace. Bake in three large pans four hours.

Stir the sugar and butter to a cream, beat the yolks and whites of the eggs separately, and add them to the butter and sugar, then by degrees put in two-thirds of the flour, then the spice and brandy or wine, and last the fruit, mixed with the remaining third of the flour. Have the citron ready cut up, and when you have put a little cake into the pan, put in a layer of citron, then more cake, and again citron and cake alternately. This quantity will bake in one cake in five hours, in two cakes, three hours. Each of these two kinds will keep years, if frosted.

Three Hebes' Lemonade

Mr. Laurence and Aunt March shrugged and smiled at one another when water, lemonade, and coffee were found to be the only sorts of nectar which the three Hebes carried round. No one said anything, however, till Laurie, who insisted on serving the bride, appeared before her, with a loaded salver in his hand and a puzzled expression on his face.

"Has Jo smashed all the bottles by accident?" he whispered, "or am I merely laboring under a delusion that I saw some lying about loose this morning?"

"No; your grandfather kindly offered us his best, and Aunt March actually sent some, but father put away a little for Beth, and despatched the rest to the Soldiers' Home. You know he thinks that wine should be used only in illness, and mother says that neither she nor her daughters will ever offer it to any young man under her roof."

CHAPTER 25: "THE FIRST WEDDING"

As Mrs. S. J. Hale noted in her 1839 cookbook, *The Good Housekeeper,* lemonade "is the best beverage for parties, cool, refreshing, pleasant, and salubrious." Perfect for Meg and John's strictly dry wedding! Small lemons with thinner skins tend to make better, more fragrant lemonade than the larger ones with thick, nubbly rinds.

Makes 4 servings

- 4 cups (1 quart) water
- 6 lemons
- ½ to 1 cup sugar
- plenty of ice, for serving

1. Measure the water into a pitcher.

2. Roll the lemons under your hand on the counter, applying pressure with the heel of your hand. (This will break down the lemons and make them easier to juice.)

3. Cut and squeeze the lemons into the water.

4. Add sugar to taste, and stir thoroughly.

5. Fill 4 glasses with ice, and pour in the lemonade.

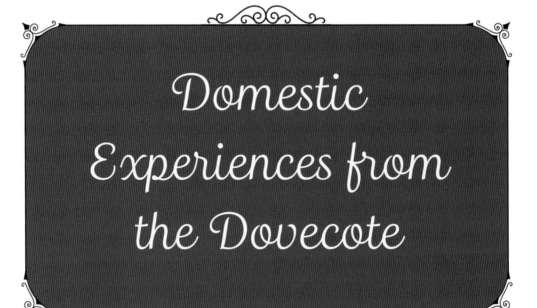

Domestic Experiences from the Dovecote

Like most other young matrons, Meg began her married life with the determination to be a model housekeeper. John should find home a paradise; he should always see a smiling face, should fare sumptuously every day, and never know the loss of a button. She brought so much love, energy, and cheerfulness to the work that she could not but succeed, in spite of some obstacles. Her paradise was not a tranquil one; for the little woman fussed, was over-anxious to please, and bustled about like a true Martha, cumbered with many cares. She was too tired, sometimes, even to smile; John grew dyspeptic after a course of dainty dishes, and ungratefully demanded plain fare.

CHAPTER 28: "DOMESTIC EXPERIENCES"

Meg and John start out their married life by "playing house," charmed by the idea of having their own household, with each trying their best to act out the role of husband or wife as they imagine they're supposed to do. Of course, real life isn't like that. Some days the jelly doesn't jell, the salary isn't enough for a new overcoat, the kids won't stay in bed, the parents forget to talk to each other ... but these small setbacks ultimately bring them closer together, and they realize they need to participate in each other's lives and be equals rather than playing roles. As Marmee tells Meg, "Talk with him, let him read to you, exchange ideas, and help each other in that way. Don't shut yourself up in a bandbox because you are a woman, but understand what is going on, and educate yourself to take your part in the world's work, for it all affects you and yours."

The book doesn't always say exactly what Meg cooked for John, but we've put together a few sample meals—the fancy-sounding Alamode Beef for Meg's ambitious phase, served with fresh summer vegetables; the frugal but tasty leftovers meal of beef hash and bread-pudding; and the slightly daring mutton curry with rice, perhaps to add some spice to the relationship?

Mathematical Mutton Curry

They were very happy, even after they discovered that they couldn't live on love alone. John did not find Meg's beauty diminished, though she beamed at him from behind the familiar coffee-pot; nor did Meg miss any of the romance from the daily parting, when her husband followed up his kiss with the tender inquiry, "Shall I send home veal or mutton for dinner, darling?" [...] While the cooking mania lasted she went through Mrs. Cornelius's Receipt Book as if it were a mathematical exercise, working out the problems with patience and care.

CHAPTER 28: "DOMESTIC EXPERIENCES"

We often think of Victorian-era food as plain and bland, and a lot of it was, but all kinds of ingredients and spices were being imported from India and Asia and were an important part of the cooking repertoire. As Meg worked her way through *The Young Housekeeper's Friend*, she would have come across this "Calcutta Curry." Mutton being hard to come by in the U.S. these days, we made the curry with lamb instead. This curry can be made ahead and will be even better the next day.

Makes 6 servings

For the curry:
- 2 pounds lamb shoulder chops
- 4 cups (1 quart) water
- 2 tablespoons butter
- 1 large onion, diced
- 2 tablespoons curry powder
  (or more to taste)
- ½ cup flour
- salt
- 1 lemon

For the rice:
- 2 cups long-grain rice
- 6 cups warm water
- 1 tablespoon salt

PREPARE THE CURRY:

1. Cut the meat off the bones of the lamb shoulder chops. Put the bones and any other trimmings in a medium saucepan with the water over medium-low heat, and let them simmer while you prepare the other ingredients. Skim off any foam that appears.

2. Chop the meat into ½-inch cubes.

3. Melt the butter in a large pot over medium-high heat, then add the onions. Sauté until the onions are browned, about 5 minutes. (While the onions are cooking, start the rice.)

4. Add the curry powder and flour, and stir to coat the onions. Keep stirring for 1 to 2 minutes, until the flour is browning and starting to stick to the bottom of the pot. Be careful not to let it burn.

5. Add the cubed lamb and stir again until everything is evenly coated with the flour mixture and the lamb is starting to brown, about 3 minutes.

6. Pour the lamb broth through a strainer into the large pot with the other ingredients. Discard the bones and other trimmings. Stir well, scraping the bottom of the pot to combine all of the curry mixture.

7. Turn the heat to low and simmer until the sauce is thickened and the lamb is cooked through; 10 minutes should be enough to cook everything, but longer is better. Add salt to taste.

8. Serve over rice, with lemon wedges to squeeze over the top or lemon catsup (page 83).

PREPARE THE RICE:

1. Rinse the rice well in a strainer.

2. Put the water and salt in a large pot.

3. Add the rice and bring to a boil over high heat.

4. Reduce to a simmer and cook, uncovered, for 10 minutes, or until the rice is tender.

5. Drain through a sieve and fluff with a fork before serving.

Friendly Advice: Not a fan of lamb? You can substitute beef, chicken, or pork, and add potatoes and carrots if you'd like to add more substance to the meal.

Frugal Bread-Pudding and Hash

An evening with John over the account-books usually produced a temporary lull in the culinary enthusiasm, and a frugal fit would ensue, during which the poor man was put through a course of bread-pudding, hash, and warmed-over coffee, which tried his soul, although he bore it with praise-worthy fortitude.

CHAPTER 28: "DOMESTIC EXPERIENCES"

Bread-Pudding

This bread-pudding is less rich and sweet than modern versions, and is even better reheated the next day. The original recipe says to flavor the custard with peach leaves, but since those aren't always available, we used almond extract.

Makes 8 servings

- 4 cups (1 quart) milk
- 5 eggs
- 1 teaspoon nutmeg
- ½ teaspoon salt
- ⅓ cup sugar
- ½ teaspoon almond extract

- 2 tablespoons butter, softened, plus more for the pan
- 5 slices hearty white bread (Good Family Bread, page 142, is a good option)
- 1 cup finely chopped dried peaches, raisins, or other dried fruit

1. Heat the milk in a medium saucepan over medium heat.

2. Beat the eggs, nutmeg, salt, and sugar together in a small bowl.

3. Once the milk starts to bubble at the edges, turn the heat off and whisk ½ cup hot milk into the egg mixture, then another ½ cup, then pour all the egg mixture into the milk in the pan.

4. Heat on low, stirring constantly, until it's thick enough to coat the back of a spoon.

5. Immediately remove from the heat and pour into a large bowl, then stir in the almond extract.

6. Butter a 9 x 9-inch baking dish and preheat the oven to 350°F.

7. Butter each slice of bread then cut them into 1-inch pieces.

8. Add the bread pieces and the dried peaches or other dried fruit to the custard and mix well.

9. Pour everything into the baking dish and cover with foil.

10. Bake about 30 minutes, or until heated through and starting to bubble.

Friendly Advice: If you have access to a peach tree in the right season, instead of adding the almond extract, try steeping a handful of young leaves in the warm milk for a few minutes (not too long, or it will be bitter) before you make the custard.

Domestic Experiences.

Beef Hash

This is by no means an elegant dish—one would certainly not serve it if Mrs. Amy Laurence were coming to dine—but it is cozy and comforting and a good way to stretch leftover roast beef into a meal. Note: In the cookbooks of this era, "hash" is usually some sort of meat-and-gravy dish, rather than the meat-fried-with-potatoes diner food that's more common today.

Makes 2 servings

- 2 tablespoons butter
- 1 small onion, diced
- 2 tablespoons flour
- 2 cups beef stock
- 1 teaspoon cider vinegar
- 1 tablespoon minced parsley (optional)
- 1 sprig of thyme (optional)
- 1½ cups diced Roast Beef for Great Appetites (page 56), preferably cooked rare
- salt and pepper
- 2 slices toast (Good Family Bread, page 142, is a good option)

1. Melt the butter in a small frying pan over medium heat.

2. Add the onions, and cook till they have softened a bit and are becoming translucent, about 5 minutes.

3. Add the flour and stir till it becomes a paste. Let it cook for 1 minute.

4. Add the beef stock a little at a time, stirring to completely incorporate each addition before adding more. You should now have a nice gravy. If it's too thick, you can add water. If too thin, let it boil a little longer.

5. Add the vinegar, parsley, and thyme, if using, and beef. Turn down the heat and let everything warm through, but don't let it boil or the meat may become tough.

6. Taste, and add salt and pepper to your liking.

7. Serve in shallow bowls ladled over toast, or with the toast on the side for dipping if you prefer.

Currant Jelly for the Family Jar

Fired with a housewifely wish to see her store-room stocked with home-made preserves, she undertook to put up her own currant jelly. John was requested to order home a dozen or so of little pots, and an extra quantity of sugar, for their own currants were ripe, and were to be attended to at once. [...] Home came four dozen delightful little pots, half a barrel of sugar, and a small boy to pick the currants for her. With her pretty hair tucked into a little cap, arms bared to the elbow, and a checked apron which had a coquettish look in spite of the bib, the young housewife fell to work, feeling no doubts about her success; for hadn't she seen Hannah do it hundreds of times? The array of pots rather amazed her at first, but John was so fond of jelly, and the nice little jars would look so well on the top shelf, that Meg resolved to fill them all, and spent a long day picking, boiling, straining, and fussing over her jelly. She did her best; she asked advice of Mrs. Cornelius; she racked her brain to remember what Hannah did that she left undone; she reboiled, resugared, and restrained, but that dreadful stuff wouldn't *"jell."*

CHAPTER 28: "DOMESTIC EXPERIENCES"

A jelly bag is nice to have for this—it's a muslin bag that hangs on a stand over a bowl, allowing the juice to drain out slowly without any pulp getting through. You can rig up a makeshift version by lining a colander with several layers of cheesecloth and setting it over a bowl.

1 pound of currants will make about 1 cup of jelly

- fresh or frozen red currants (not dried)
- white sugar to equal the weight of the juice from the currants

1. Rinse the currants and put them in a saucepan that would hold about twice their volume—stems, seeds, and all. Add a little water in the bottom of the pan, about ½ inch deep.

2. Set up the jelly bag over a bowl.

3. Cook the currants over medium heat, mashing with a potato masher or the back of a spoon, until the berries have released their juice. This will only take a few minutes.

4. Transfer the currants and juice to the jelly bag, and let it drain for several hours or overnight. Don't wring out the bag, or the jelly will be cloudy.

5. When you're ready to start cooking, put a small plate in the freezer.

6. Weigh the juice that drained out, and add the same weight of sugar.

7. Transfer the juice and sugar mixture to a saucepan and set it over medium heat.

8. Bring to a strong boil, with lots of bubbles all over the surface (but don't let it boil over).

9. Reduce heat to low and boil for 5 to 10 minutes, stirring often, until you can see it starting to thicken a bit when you let it run off the spoon, or until it reaches 220°F on a candy thermometer (an instant-read or laser thermometer doesn't work well for this).

10. Test the jelly by dropping a small spoonful on the cold plate and putting it back in the freezer for 1 minute. Take it out again and push your finger through the jelly on the plate. If it wrinkles as you push it, it's done. If not, keep boiling and try again in a few minutes.

11. Once done, transfer the jelly to a jar through a fine-mesh strainer and process it for canning if you like, or just store it in the refrigerator (it will last for up to three months).

Friendly Advice: Making jelly is easy—it's just equal weights of juice and sugar, so you almost don't need a recipe. Currants have a lot of pectin, so they should jell up nicely, despite poor Meg's difficulties. Mrs. Cornelius warns that you shouldn't stop boiling the jelly once you've started—maybe that was Meg's problem?

The Beef and Vegetables John Sent Home

"A man to dinner, and everything in a mess! John Brooke, how *could* you do such a thing?"

"I didn't know it this morning, and there was no time to send word, for I met him on the way out. I never thought of asking leave, when you have always told me to do as I liked. I never tried it before, and hang me if I ever do again!" added John, with an aggrieved air.

"I should hope not! Take him away at once; I can't see him, and there isn't any dinner."

"Well, I like that! Where's the beef and vegetables I sent home, and the pudding you promised?" cried John, rushing to the larder.

CHAPTER 28: "DOMESTIC EXPERIENCES"

Alamode Beef

Alamode beef is a recipe that Meg might have picked out as a new housekeeper, since it sounds fancy (though it's not correct French), but it's not too challenging. This dish is like a stuffed pot roast, but seasoned with cloves.

Makes 3 or 4 servings

- 1 cup fresh bread crumbs
- 3 ounces finely chopped salt pork
- 1 teaspoon freshly ground pepper
- ½ teaspoon ground cloves
- 1 tablespoon minced fresh marjoram

- 2½ pounds 2-inch-thick round steak
- 1½ ounces cubed salt pork
- 1 large onion, chopped
- 5 or 6 whole cloves
- ¼ cup plus 1 tablespoon flour

1. To prepare the stuffing, combine the bread crumbs, finely chopped salt pork, pepper, ground cloves, and marjoram in a small bowl, and set aside.

2. Trim off any strips of fat on the edge of the steak, and lay it flat on a cutting board.

3. Slice a 1-inch cross-hatch pattern into the beef, stopping short of cutting all the way through.

4. Push the stuffing into the incisions in the beef, and spread the rest across the top.

5. Roll the beef up, fasten with skewers, and secure with twine.

6. In a Dutch oven, fry the cubed salt pork over medium heat. Cook until the fat is rendered and the salt pork pieces are crispy, like bacon. Remove the cubes, leaving the liquid fat. Turn the heat to high, and brown all sides of the beef, about 2 minutes per side.

7. Add water until the beef is just covered. Add the chopped onion and whole cloves. Boil uncovered, steadily but gently, for 3 to 4 hours. The liquid should reduce, but make sure it doesn't burn. Roll the beef over every now and then so that one side doesn't dry out.

8. While the beef is boiling, brown the flour. Preheat the oven to 400°F. Spread the flour on a cast-iron skillet and bake for 20 to 25 minutes, stirring with a wooden spoon every 7 minutes, until the flour is a toasty brown, like the color of bran flakes. Remove from the skillet. (Cool completely before storing in a container—it'll keep in the fridge for 2 months.)

9. Take out the beef. If you would like to thicken the broth into gravy, raise the heat to high.

10. Place a ladleful of the broth in a small heatproof bowl, and mix in browned flour, 2 tablespoons per cup of broth. Add to the pot, mix, and bring to a boil. Once the gravy is thickened, take it off the heat, add the meat back to the pot, and cover until dinnertime.

11. Serve in slices with gravy on the side.

Summary Squash

The original recipe says to "boil it whole, in a little bag kept for the purpose." The bag isn't really necessary, but squeezing out the water this way concentrates and improves the flavor of the squash. Look for squash with thin, tender skin.

Makes 4 servings

- 2 large yellow crookneck squash or 4 zucchini, about 1 pound
- 1 tablespoon butter
- salt

1. Put the squash whole into a large pot with enough water to cover.

2. Boil for 45 minutes (less if you have smaller squash), until very tender.

3. Remove the squash and put into a colander.

4. Use a smaller bowl to press out most of the liquid from the squash.

5. Transfer into a serving bowl, add butter and season to taste with salt, and mash well with a fork.

String Beans

You might think it sounds strange to add flour at the end, but it makes a nice sauce for the beans. Cutting them in little pieces also improves the dish; it seems to bring out the flavor of the beans.

Makes 4 servings

- 1 pound string beans
- ½ teaspoon salt
- 2 tablespoons softened butter
- 2 tablespoons flour

1. Remove the ends of the beans, and cut them into ½-inch pieces.

2. Place in a medium saucepan with the salt and just enough water to barely cover.

3. Boil over high heat until bright green and tender, 5 to 10 minutes.

4. Turn the heat to low, add the butter and flour, and stir well until the sauce thickens, 1 to 2 minutes.

Meg

Demi's Little Cakes

Meg slipped away, and ran down to greet her husband with a smiling face, and the little blue bow in her hair which was his especial admiration. He saw it at once and said with pleased surprise,—"Why, little mother, how gay we are tonight. Do you expect company?"

"Only you, dear."

"Is it a birthday, anniversary, or anything?"

"No; I'm tired of being dowdy, so I dressed up as a change. You always make yourself nice for table, no matter how tired you are; so why shouldn't I when I have the time?"

"I do it out of respect for you, my dear," said old-fashioned John.

"Ditto, ditto, Mr. Brooke," laughed Meg, looking young and pretty again, as she nodded to him over the teapot.

"Well, it's altogether delightful, and like old times. This tastes right. I drink your health, dear." And John sipped his tea with an air of reposeful rapture, which was of very short duration, however; for, as he put down his cup, the door-handle rattled mysteriously, and a little voice was heard, saying impatiently,—

"Opy doy; me's tummin!"

"It's that naughty boy. I told him to go to sleep alone, and here he is, downstairs, getting his death a-cold pattering over that canvas," said Meg, answering the call.

"Mornin' now," announced Demi in joyful tone, as he entered, with his long night-gown gracefully festooned over his arm, and every curl bobbing gayly as he pranced about the table, eyeing the "cakies" with loving glances.

"No, it isn't morning yet. You must go to bed, and not trouble poor mamma; then you can have the little cake with sugar on it."

CHAPTER 38: "ON THE SHELF"

These turn out fluffy and lemony; they would serve equally well as a nice dessert for a romantic evening or a bribe for a toddler who won't stay in bed.

Makes 12 cupcakes

- ½ cup butter
- ¼ teaspoon salt
- 1 cup sugar, plus more for sprinkling
- 2 whole eggs plus 1 egg yolk
- zest and juice of ½ lemon
- 1¾ cups flour
- ½ cup buttermilk
- ½ teaspoon baking soda

1. Have all the ingredients at room temperature.

2. Preheat the oven to 350°F and line a muffin tin with paper liners.

3. In the bowl of a stand mixer fitted with the paddle attachment, cream the butter, salt and sugar together until well combined.

4. Add the eggs and lemon zest. Whip on high speed for 3 to 5 minutes, until it's light-colored and fluffy.

5. Add half the flour, mix, then add the buttermilk, mix, then add the rest of the flour with the baking soda.

6. Add the lemon juice and stir to combine.

7. Portion the batter into the muffin cups. Fill only three-quarters full.

8. Lightly grease the top of the muffin tin in case they spill over.

9. Bake about 18 minutes, until the tops are set and edges are just browning.

10. Immediately after removing them from the oven, sprinkle the tops with sugar.

Meg

CHAPTER 2

Jo

But you see, Jo wasn't a heroine; she was only a struggling human girl like hundreds of others, and she just acted out her nature, being sad, cross, listless, or energetic, as the mood suggested.

Chapter 42: "All Alone"

Jo is probably your favorite, and why wouldn't she be? She's talented, literary, kind-hearted, loyal, and generous, but just like a real person she's also bad-tempered, impatient, headstrong, and in a constant state of chaos. Who doesn't relate to that?

It's no surprise that generations of little women have identified with Jo's struggle to fit herself into the conventional image of femininity—the ideal is always changing, and always unattainable. She is absolutely incapable of being anything other than authentic at all times, which is both endearing and frustrating for those who love her. She's constantly getting in her own way, saying the wrong thing at the worst possible time, and scandalizing polite society with her lack of manners, boyish appearance, and general inability to act like a proper young lady.

On the other hand, Jo does have domestic skills—she sews most of her sisters' dresses, and is an excellent wrangler of children. With her father away in the war, she calls herself the "man of the family" and does her best to look after her mother and sisters. When Beth is ill, Jo stays by her side night and day, caring for her tenderly until the end. Jo may be topsy-turvy, but underneath everything, she's a total softie; as Meg says, "like a chestnut burr, prickly outside, but silky-soft within, and a sweet kernel, if one can only get at it."

Eating is simply a practicality for Jo; she only learns to cook because it's necessary for basic survival. She'll occasionally take on a cooking project as a personal challenge, but Jo doesn't have the patience and foresight required to pull off anything fancy. We can see modern-day Jo living a happy, gender-nonconforming life with her kitchen cupboards full of books and half-finished projects, and her freezer stuffed with homemade meals from Beth and Marmee because she is one of those people who always forgets to eat. Amy drags her out to try the latest food trends, but Jo's too busy thinking about her students or her writing to notice what she's eating, and anyway, she'd prefer a nice crisp apple to any elaborate patisserie.

The recipes in Jo's chapter are straightforward, tasty, and useful—like gingerbread nuts for quieting noisy children. There's a menu for a festive dinner party: Jo's attempt is such a disaster that it becomes a family joke, but with modernized recipes and the benefit of our experience, you can pull it off easily. And the cozy, nourishing boarding house dinner that ends in an any-season peach pie showcases simple flavors in a way that our modern palates don't often experience ... not to mention, it makes great brain fuel for writing about gruesome murders and tragic romances.

Molasses Candy Fit to Eat

> "Don't try too many messes, Jo, for you can't make anything but gingerbread and molasses candy, fit to eat."
>
> CHAPTER 11: "EXPERIMENTS"

Jo's not the best of cooks, and when she starts getting carried away by grand plans for a dinner, Meg reminds her that her repertoire is very limited. It's impressive to us that of all things, Jo can make molasses candy, since it takes cooking instinct and experience to figure out the timing for boiling and pulling it. Make sure to have a few friends around to help pull the candy, and use plenty of butter on your hands to keep from burning yourself!

Makes about 40 pieces

- ½ to 1 cup (1 to 2 sticks) softened butter
- 1 cup molasses
- 4½ tablespoons brown sugar
- zest and juice of 1 lemon
- ¼ cup blanched slivered almonds

1. Before you start, generously butter a square casserole dish or pie pan. Make sure the dish has been warmed a little and is not cold.

2. Pour the molasses and brown sugar in a large saucepan (bigger than you think you need, as it will boil up) on medium-high heat. Clip a candy thermometer to the side of the saucepan.

3. Bring to a boil, stirring constantly, and reduce the heat to low. Continue to stir until the mixture reaches the hard ball stage (250°F to 265°F), and then remove from heat.

4. Slowly add lemon juice while stirring—if you add it too quickly, it can rise rapidly. Once it's mixed in, stir in the zest and almonds.

5. Pour the mixture into the buttered dish and allow it to cool for 6 to 10 minutes. In the meantime, call in at least three helpers, and have them wash and rinse their hands thoroughly until they no longer smell like soap. Coat all of your hands in a good layer of butter.

6. Once the candy has cooled enough, it should move in one big mass but be soft enough to pull. It will be almost too hot to hold.

7. Give everyone a hunk of the candy and have them pull it, folding it over, and then pulling again, until it turns lighter in color.

8. When the candy gets too hard to pull, stretch it into ropes about 1 inch thick, and cut into pieces with buttered kitchen scissors.

Friendly Advice: The more you pull, the lighter it will be, the nicer the flavor, and the softer to chew. Pull fast and furiously! Don't give up too early!

Get the Receipt

If you want to do it the old-fashioned way and cook over a fire for 3 hours, try this recipe from Eliza Leslie's *Directions for Cookery, In Its Various Branches* (1840):

Mix a pound of the best brown sugar with two quarts of West India molasses, (which must be perfectly sweet), and boil it in a preserving kettle over a moderate fire for three hours, skimming it well, and stirring it frequently after the scum has ceased to rise; taking care that it does not burn. Have ready the grated rind and the juice of three lemons, and stir them into the molasses after it has boiled about two hours and a half; or you may substitute a large tea-spoonful of strong essence of lemon. The flavor of the lemon will all be boiled out if it is put in too soon. The mixture should boil at least three hours, that it may be crisp and brittle when cold. If it is taken off the fire too soon, or before it has boiled sufficiently, it will not congeal, but will be tough and ropy, and must be boiled over again. It will cease boiling of itself when it is thoroughly done. Then take it off the fire; have ready a square tin pan; put the mixture into it, and set it away to cool.

You may make molasses candy with almonds blanched and slit into pieces; stir them in by degrees after the mixture has boiled two hours and a half. Or you may blanch a quart of ground-nuts and put them in instead of the almonds.

Gingerbread Nuts for Roars

New York, November

Dear Marmee and Beth,—

I'm going to write you a regular volume, for I've got heaps to tell, though I'm not a fine young lady traveling on the continent. When I lost sight of father's dear old face, I felt a trifle blue, and might have shed a briny drop or two, if an Irish lady with four small children, all crying more or less, hadn't diverted my mind; for I amused myself by dropping gingerbread nuts over the seat every time they opened their mouths to roar.

CHAPTER 33: "JO'S JOURNAL"

These are somewhere between *Pfeffernüsse* (which literally means "pepper-nuts" in German) and gingersnaps (which are still often called ginger nuts in the UK). Some recipes tell you to roll them out and cut them into thin circles, which you certainly can do, but we think they're much cuter this way. Just right for distracting a grouchy child on a train trip.

Makes more than 100 tiny cookies

- ½ cup molasses
- ½ cup (1 stick) butter
- ⅓ cup sugar
- ½ teaspoon salt
- 2¼ cups flour
- ¼ teaspoon baking soda
- 1 tablespoon ground ginger
- ½ teaspoon ground cinnamon
- ¼ teaspoon ground cloves

Friendly Advice: It's not in the original recipe, but if you like, you can roll the balls in sugar before putting them on the baking sheet. It gives them a nice crunchy crust.

1. Combine the molasses, butter, and sugar in a medium saucepan over medium heat, and warm until the molasses bubbles at the edges and the butter is mostly melted, about 5 minutes.

2. Allow to cool slightly, while you combine the rest of the ingredients in a large bowl.

3. Pour the molasses mixture into the dry ingredients and stir well to combine. You should have a fairly thick dough that will hold its shape when rolled in a small ball.

4. Preheat the oven to 350°F.

5. Roll the dough into ½-inch balls, about the size of a marble. Place them about ½ inch apart on a baking sheet, then poke the top of each one with your fingertip to flatten it slightly (boop!) and leave a little dip in the middle. They won't spread much while cooking.

6. Bake for 8 to 15 minutes, depending on how you like your cookies. The shorter time will give you a softer, doughier result, and the longer time will produce a hard, crunchy cookie with a nice roasty taste. We couldn't decide which one we preferred—try both!

Old-Fashioned Measurements

Nineteenth-century cookbooks often list old-fashioned measurements, which are quaint and fun to read, but not terribly helpful if you're trying to actually cook from them. We've made all the necessary modifications for the recipes in this book, but if you're ever looking to try your hand at a vintage recipe, here's a list of conversions for some of the most common terms:

- 60 drops = 1 teaspoon of liquid
- Butter the size of a nut or walnut = 2 tablespoons
- Butter the size of an egg = ½ cup
- Coffee cup = 1 cup
- Dash = ⅛ teaspoon
- Dessert spoon = 2 teaspoons
- Gill = ½ cup
- Lump of butter = 2 tablespoons
- Pinch = 1/16 teaspoon
- Salt spoon = ¼ teaspoon
- Teacup = ¾ cup
- Tin cup = 1 cup
- Tumblerful = 2 cups
- Wineglass = ¼ cup

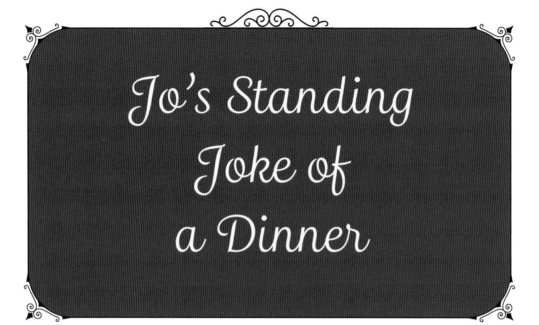

Jo's Standing Joke of a Dinner

Despair seized them, when, a few minutes later, Miss Crocker appeared, and said she'd come to dinner. Now, this lady was a thin, yellow spinster, with a sharp nose, and inquisitive eyes, who saw everything, and gossiped about all she saw. They disliked her, but had been taught to be kind to her, simply because she was old and poor, and had few friends. So Meg gave her the easy-chair, and tried to entertain her, while she asked questions, criticised everything, and told stories of the people whom she knew.

Language cannot describe the anxieties, experiences, and exertions which Jo underwent that morning; and the dinner she served up became a standing joke. Fearing to ask any more advice, she did her best alone, and discovered that something more than energy and good-will is necessary to make a cook. [...]

Poor Jo would gladly have gone under the table, as one thing after another was tasted and left; while Amy giggled, Meg looked distressed, Miss Crocker pursed her lips, and Laurie talked and laughed with all his might, to give a cheerful tone to the festive scene. [...]

[Jo] turned scarlet, and was on the verge of crying, when she met Laurie's eyes, which *would* look merry in spite of his heroic efforts; the comical side of the affair suddenly struck her, and she laughed till the tears ran down her cheeks. So did every one else, even "Croaker," as the girls called the old lady; and the unfortunate dinner ended gayly, with bread and butter, olives and fun.

CHAPTER 11: "EXPERIMENTS"

We've all been there: At one point or another, we've gotten overconfident, invited a bunch of guests over, promised an impressive feast that's beyond our skill ... and ended up with an embarrassing, inedible waste of ingredients and time, along with a kitchen covered in dirty dishes and cooking residue. We feel your pain, Jo!

We do admire Jo's taste in menu planning, even though she didn't have the expertise or experience to match her vision. This is a great, well-rounded meal for friends—a comforting, nourishing treat without being overly fancy. Jo's standing joke of a dinner features corned beef, boiled potatoes, asparagus, lobster salad, bread (page 142) and butter, blanc-mange (page 114), and strawberries and cream.

Corned Beef

"Well, they can eat beef, and bread and butter, if they are hungry; only it's mortifying to have to spend your whole morning for nothing," thought Jo, as she rang the bell half an hour later than usual, and stood, hot, tired, and dispirited, surveying the feast spread for Laurie, accustomed to all sorts of elegance, and Miss Crocker, whose curious eyes would mark all failures, and whose tattling tongue would report them far and wide.

CHAPTER 11: "EXPERIMENTS"

The "corn" in corned beef actually refers to the kernels of salt that were used to preserve it—there's no corn in it at all! Nowadays most corned beef is brined with a variety of spices, but recipes from the 19th century just used salt, saltpeter (similar to modern curing salt), water, and sometimes molasses. We were surprised to find that this version doesn't taste much different from the modern spiced one—you do taste the molasses, but it's not sweet and it still has the distinctive corned beef flavor and color.

Before refrigeration, you would be careful to only make this when the weather was cool, but now we have a handy eternal winter in the refrigerator and can happily make corned beef in July if we feel like it.

Makes 6 to 8 servings

- 8 cups (2 quarts) water
- 1½ cups salt
- 2 tablespoons pink curing salt
- ½ cup molasses
- 1 beef brisket, about 5 pounds

- 4 cups ice
- 2 bay leaves (optional)
- 1 teaspoon black peppercorns (optional)
- carrots, potatoes, cabbage, for serving (optional)

AT LEAST 10 DAYS BEFORE YOU WANT TO EAT:

(If you have an already-corned beef, skip ahead to the cooking stage.)

1. Combine the water, salt, pink curing salt, and molasses in a large stock pot that will hold the brisket and will fit in your refrigerator. Heat on high until the salt and molasses are dissolved, then remove from heat and allow to cool.

2. Rinse the brisket and trim off some of the fat cap if you like, but leave a ½-inch layer at least. Trim off any silver skin or gristle on the outside.

3. Add the ice to the brine in the pot, and stir until the mixture is completely cold.

4. Put the brisket in the pot, making sure it's completely submerged. If it wants to float, place a ceramic bowl or other heavy, nonreactive object on top to keep it under the brine.

5. Put the whole contraption in the refrigerator and leave it for 10 to 14 days (go for the longer end if your brisket is especially thick). Check on it every day or so and flip the meat over so it brines evenly.

WHEN YOU ARE READY TO COOK THE BEEF:

1. Pour off the brine and rinse the brisket well. Wash the pot.

2. Return the brisket to the clean pot and fill it with enough water to cover the meat by an inch or so. Add the bay leaves and peppercorns, if using.

3. Simmer over low heat so the water is barely bubbling for about 5 hours, until fork-tender, or 145°F in the center of the brisket. Check occasionally and add more water as needed.

4. In the last 30 minutes of cooking, you can add vegetables if you like, starting with carrots, then potatoes, then cabbage.

Lobster Salad

The salad-dressing so aggravated her, that she let everything else go till she had convinced herself that she could not make it fit to eat. The lobster was a scarlet mystery to her, but she hammered and poked, till it was unshelled, and its meagre proportions concealed in a grove of lettuce-leaves.

CHAPTER 11: "EXPERIMENTS"

This makes an elegant presentation of lettuce topped with lobster and drizzled with a creamy, tangy sauce. Despite Jo's aggravation, the dressing is particularly good, and also goes well on the boiled potatoes (or eaten with a spoon).

One small lobster will serve about two people. Adjust the water and salt as needed depending on how many you're serving. Note: Lobsters must be alive when you cook them. Don't put ice on them or put them in fresh water—this will kill them.

Makes 2 servings

For the dressing:

- 4 eggs
- 3 tablespoons olive oil
- ⅓ cup white vinegar
- 1 teaspoon freshly ground pepper
- 1 tablespoon whole-grain mustard
- ½ teaspoon salt
- fresh lemon juice to taste (optional)

For the salad:

- 3 quarts (12 cups) water
- 3 tablespoons salt
- 1 small lobster (1½ to 2 pounds) per two people, or however many you can afford
- cool water (3 quarts per 1½ to 2 pounds of lobster)
- salt (1 tablespoon for every quart of water)
- 6 to 8 leaves butter lettuce
- freshly ground pepper for every pound of lobster

PREPARE THE DRESSING:

1. Cover the eggs with cold water in a large saucepan over high heat. Turn the heat off as soon as the water comes to a full boil. Let the eggs sit in the hot water to cook fully, 15 minutes to get to hard-boiled.

2. Take out the egg yolks, allow them to cool, and mash them in a small bowl.

Discard the whites or use them to decorate the salad.

3. Add olive oil, vinegar, mustard, freshly ground pepper, and salt in small increments to taste. Fresh lemon juice isn't in the original recipe, but it's very nice with the lobster. Add it as desired.

PREPARE THE SALAD:

1. Bring the water and salt (1 tablespoon per quart) to a rolling boil in a pot large enough that the lobster will be fully submerged and have a bit of extra room. If you would like to kill the lobster humanely, place the lobster in the freezer for 10 minutes, right before cooking.

2. Drop the lobster in the water headfirst, using tongs. Don't cover the pot.

3. Stir the lobster halfway through boiling. Boiled lobsters will be bright red when done. Boiling times depend on the weight of the total amount of lobster you have (not individual weight):

- 1 pound: 5 to 7 minutes
- 1¼ pounds: 7 to 8 minutes
- 1½ pounds: 8 to 10 minutes
- 2 pounds: 10 to 12 minutes
- 3 pounds: 12 to 14 minutes

4. Place the boiled lobsters in cool water until they are cool enough to crack and remove the meat.

5. Dice the lobster meat and arrange it on the lettuce leaves.

6. Drizzle the dressing over the lobster, and serve with freshly ground pepper.

Jo

Plenty of Potatoes

The potatoes had to be hurried, not to keep the asparagus waiting, and were not done at last.

A nice simple boiled potato with plenty of butter is a satisfying side ... as long as you cook them all the way through.

Makes 4 servings

- 4 large russet potatoes or 8 small waxy potatoes
- 2 tablespoons salt
- water
- butter, for the table

1. Peel the potatoes if you prefer, and cut them in halves or quarters depending on size.

2. Put the potatoes in a large pot with the salt and fill the pot three-quarters full with water.

3. Heat on high until it comes to a boil, then reduce to medium and boil until the potatoes are tender, 15 to 25 minutes. Check for doneness by pulling one out and cutting it in half to see if the middle is cooked through.

4. Drain the water off, and shake the potatoes in the pot over medium-high heat to let them dry, then serve with butter as you like.

Boiled Asparagus

She boiled the asparagus for an hour, and was grieved to find the heads cooked off and the stalks harder than ever.

CHAPTER II: "EXPERIMENTS"

When we first read this recipe in *The Young Housekeeper's Friend*, we could not imagine how it would be anything more than a giant pile of mush. But once we tasted it, we were amazed—each ingredient contributes something and it all adds up to delicious. The original version has you tie the asparagus in little bundles with string, but it's not really necessary. Everything else is just as Mrs. Cornelius said.

Makes 4 servings

- 1 pound asparagus, tough ends snapped off
- 1 tablespoon salt
- 4 slices sturdy white bread
- 2 tablespoons softened butter

1. Put the asparagus in a large pot over high heat, with the salt and enough water to cover by about an inch. Boil until quite soft, 15 to 25 minutes, depending how thick the asparagus are.

2. While the asparagus is cooking, toast the bread.

3. Have four small plates and the softened butter handy.

4. When the asparagus is nearly done (overcooked by modern standards), quickly dip each slice of bread into the asparagus water, lay it on the plate, and spread it with butter.

5. Lay a portion of asparagus on each slice of bread, dot with a tiny bit more butter, and serve.

6. Eat with knife and fork.

Friendly Advice: Make sure your asparagus is fresh, and get the best bread and butter you can—it makes all the difference. Good Family Bread (page 142) works well, or opt for a crusty artisan loaf.

Jo

Mrs. Kirke's Five O'Clock Dinner

"Mrs. Kirke asked me if I wouldn't go down to the five o'clock dinner; and, feeling a little bit homesick, I thought I would, just to see what sort of people are under the same roof with me …. [Mrs. Kirke] gave me a seat by her, and after my face cooled off, I plucked up courage, and looked about me. [...]

"Cast away at the very bottom of the table was the Professor, shouting answers to the questions of a very inquisitive, deaf old gentleman on one side, and talking philosophy with a Frenchman on the other. If Amy had been here, she'd have turned her back on him forever, because, sad to relate, he had a great appetite, and shovelled in his dinner in a manner which would have horrified 'her ladyship'. I didn't mind, for I like 'to see folks eat with a relish', as Hannah says, and the poor man must have needed a deal of food after teaching idiots all day."

CHAPTER 33: "JO'S JOURNAL"

Jo sets out for a winter in New York, anxious to see and learn new things (and to take a break from Laurie, who's obviously into her in a way she can't reciprocate). She's signed up for a job as a governess and seamstress at a boarding house, which is like a dorm for strangers in the city. Jo's lucky in her choice of employer, Mrs. Kirke, who's a friend of Marmee's and a kindly woman who makes her feel right at home. Boarding house landladies aren't usually known for their generosity or delicious food, but Mrs. Kirke seems to be an exception.

Jo doesn't describe what exactly they eat, but we can take a good guess at what they might have had for a 5 o'clock dinner in November. Mrs. Kirke would've probably provided some boarding house staples but added variety with a few more seasonal vegetables. Beef was ubiquitous on the common dining table, especially as a simple roast, stew, or steak, since poultry was expensive and a pain to prep. There was often pie, but fresh fruit was hard to come by, especially in late fall,[4] so give this dried peach pie a try. Boarding houses were known for their bad table manners,[5] so the best way to enjoy this dinner is to forget about being polite, shovel down your food, and eat with a relish!

---

4 Wendy Gamber, *The Boardinghouse in Nineteenth-Century America* (Baltimore: Johns Hopkins University Press, 2007), 79.
5 Gamber, *The Boardinghouse,* 92.

Roast Beef for Great Appetites

Makes 6 to 8 servings

- 1 boneless rump roast, 3 to 4 pounds
- 2 tablespoons kosher salt
- ¼ cup lard or bacon fat, melted
- ¼ cup flour

1. Tie the roast with string to make it an even shape and prevent some parts from cooking faster than others. Butchers will sometimes do this for you if you ask!

2. Pat the beef dry and rub with the salt.

3. Leave uncovered in the fridge for a few hours or overnight if possible.

4. Place an oven rack in the second position from the bottom. It is also helpful to take the top rack of the oven out to make room. Preheat the oven to 225°F.

5. Set a wire rack in a rimmed baking sheet.

6. Melt the lard or bacon fat in a small saucepan and keep it handy, along with a basting brush.

7. Brush the rack with lard to keep the beef from sticking.

8. Place the beef, fat cap up, on the rack. Baste it with lard, then put it in the oven.

9. Every 20 minutes, baste the meat again with the lard.

10. Roast until the internal temperature at the thickest part reaches 120°F to 125°F, 60 to 90 minutes depending on the thickness of your roast. (This should give you a medium-rare roast, 130°F to 135°F, after the browning process. If you like yours more done, roast longer.)

11. Remove the roast from the oven and sprinkle it generously all over with flour, then baste again.

12. Switch the oven to broil, and broil the roast all over, turning as needed, until the flour froths up and browns slightly.

13. At this point, if you're feeling brave, and if there are some nice drippings in the pan, you can try an exciting historical gravy method: Boil a cup or two of water and pour it slowly over the roast, washing the browned flour off into the pan below. Then remove the roast and rack and put the pan on the stove, and cook the liquid with the flour, stirring constantly, until thickened. Add salt and pepper as needed. If you're not used to making gravy, however, we would skip this step.

14. Transfer the roast to a cutting board and let it rest for a few minutes before slicing. Try to slice against the grain of the meat.

Friendly Advice: Do you have leftovers? Use them to make a beef hash (page 32) the next day!

Tomato Catsup

There used to be many kinds of ketchup/catsup, including lemon, mushroom, and walnut! They were all meant to add savory and/or acidic flavor to various dishes. For some reason, only the tomato version has survived to the present day (with a lot of sugar added), and it's so common we hardly even notice what it tastes like. It's worth making your own at least once—it will make you think of ketchup in a completely different way.

Makes about ½ cup

- 3 pounds tomatoes
- 1½ teaspoons salt
- ¼ medium onion, sliced very thin
- ¼ teaspoon ground ginger
- ¼ teaspoon ground cloves
- ¼ teaspoon ground allspice
- ¼ teaspoon pepper

1. Slice the tomatoes and sprinkle them with a little of the salt.

2. Place them in a medium saucepan with the onions and simmer, uncovered, on very low heat for 1 hour. Stir occasionally.

3. Push the tomatoes through a coarse sieve, leaving behind the skins and seeds.

4. Return the pulp to the pot, and add the ginger, cloves, allspice, pepper, and the rest of the salt.

5. Simmer for about another 20 minutes, stirring often, until it has reduced to a thick paste.

Mashed Turnips

These days, many people have never eaten a turnip, and most likely think of them as the sort of thing characters in fairytales trade for magic beans. But they are in fact delicious either raw or cooked, with an unusual sweet and sharp flavor similar to a radish. Choose the smaller ones; they're more tender. Mashed turnips make an interesting alternative to mashed potatoes if you're looking for something less starchy.

Makes 4 servings

- 2 pounds turnips, peeled and quartered
- salt
- 3 tablespoons butter

1. Put the turnips, enough cold water to cover them, and a few tablespoons of salt in a large pot.

2. Turn the stove on high. When the water begins boiling, reduce to medium-high and cook, covered, for 30 minutes or until the turnips are very tender.

3. Drain and press the water out. Mash the turnips very well with a potato masher. There may be some stringy bits stuck in the masher—don't put them back in with the turnips!

4. Add the butter and salt to taste.

Friendly Advice: If there's excess water after draining, put the mash back into the pot over medium-high heat for 2 to 3 minutes, stirring constantly to keep it from burning, until the extra liquid has cooked off.

Stewed Onions to Eat with a Relish

This dish seems to have had a bad reputation—places like boarding houses and tenements were often described as smelling unpleasantly of stewed onions, and nowadays it's difficult to find much mention of it in cookbooks at all. This version, on the other hand, is delicious and even delicate; the onions become sweet and tender, a perfect side for a Sunday roast.

Makes 4 servings

- 14 ounces small white boiling onions (pearl or cippolini onions will also work)
- ⅓ cup water, plus more for boiling the onions
- ⅓ cup milk
- 1 tablespoon butter
- salt and pepper

1. Cut off the tops and bottoms of the onions, and pull off as much skin as comes off easily.

2. In a medium pot, start the onions in enough cold salted water to cover, and boil for 20 minutes, until translucent.

3. Drain completely, and remove any remaining skins.

4. Return the onions to the pot. Add ⅓ cup water, milk, and another pinch of salt. Simmer, uncovered, over low heat for 20 minutes, until the liquid is thickened a bit but not curdled.

5. Add the butter, and season to taste with salt and pepper.

Dried Peach Pie

Why restrict yourself to peach pie only in the summer? Dried peaches are made from fruit at the peak of ripeness, and the drying process seems to concentrate the pectin, resulting in a pie that holds together nicely and has an intense peach flavor.

Makes 6 servings

- 1 pound dried peaches, diced
- zest of 1 lemon
- pinch of salt
- 2 tablespoons sugar, or to taste, plus more for sprinkling
- lemon juice, as needed
- 1 Double Pie Crust (see page 63) or store-bought pie crust
- 1 egg, beaten

PREPARE THE FILLING:

1. Combine the peaches with about double their volume of water in a large saucepan and bring to a boil.

2. As soon as it comes to a boil, remove from heat and add the lemon zest and salt.

3. Let the peaches sit for 30 minutes or so, stirring occasionally, until they have absorbed most of the water.

4. Taste and add sugar and/or lemon juice as needed—depending on the type of peaches you have, they may be more sweet or more sour.

5. Let the peach mixture cool completely while you prepare the pie crust. (Or you can make the filling ahead and refrigerate it.) You may need to add more water—there should be some juice, but it should be thick, not watery.

ASSEMBLE AND BAKE THE PIE:

1. Preheat the oven to 400°F and set a rack in the lowest position.

2. Divide the pie dough in half and roll each half into a disk about ¼-inch thick.

3. Lay the bottom crust in a 9-inch pie pan and spoon in the filling.

4. Lay the top crust over the filling and crimp the edges tightly. If you're feeling fancy, you can make a lattice crust, but a plain one works just fine here.

5. Brush the top crust with the beaten egg, then sprinkle generously with sugar.

6. If you're not making a lattice, cut vents in the crust with a small knife.

7. Bake on the lowest rack in the oven until the crust is golden brown, about 30 minutes. If the edges are cooking too quickly, cover them with foil.

8. Allow to cool before serving.

Friendly Advice: Though it's not part of the original recipe, adding a few dried apricots in the mix, about ½ cup, gives an extra layer of complexity, and whipped cream flavored with almond extract is an excellent accompaniment.

Double Pie Crust

Makes 2 (9-inch) pie crusts

- 2½ cups plus 2 tablespoons flour, divided
- 1 cup (2 sticks) plus 1 tablespoon butter, chilled and diced, divided
- ¼ cup ice water

1. In a large bowl, combine 2½ cups of the flour and the salt.

2. Cut the 1 cup diced butter into the flour (either with two knives or with your fingertips) until it resembles coarse crumbs.

3. Stir in the ice water, 1 tablespoon at a time, until the mixture forms a ball.

4. Roll out the dough and spread 1 tablespoon of butter, shaved into thin strips using a vegetable peeler, over the dough. Sprinkle the remaining 2 tablespoons of flour over the butter shavings.

5. Roll the dough up into a scroll, and then fold in half and press together. Wrap dough in plastic and refrigerate for 1 hour before rolling out.

Get the Receipt

Here is some of Mrs. Cornelius's excellent advice on making pastry (you'll notice that soggy bottoms were a concern back then just like today):

- There is hardly another article of food in which so much is sacrificed to appearance as in pastry. Everybody likes a light crust, a little brown, and not excessively rich, better than one that is half butter or lard, and baked white.

- The best-looking pastry is made with lard, but it is not so healthy or good, as that which is made with half or two thirds butter.

- It is difficult to make flaky crust in warm weather. But cooling the butter and water with ice, and having the pastry-table in the cellar, will insure tolerable success.

- A clammy lower-crust is neither good or digestible. Therefore never fill pies made of moist materials until just before putting them into the oven.

Seed-Cakes for the "Nargerie"

When I got back to the nursery there was such an uproar in the parlor that I looked in; and there was Mr. Bhaer down on his hands and knees, with Tina on his back, Kitty leading him with a jump-rope, and Minnie feeding two small boys with seed-cakes, as they roared and ramped in cages built of chairs.

"We are playing *nargerie*," explained Kitty.

"Dis is mine effalunt!" added Tina, holding on by the Professor's hair.

"Mamma always allows us to do what we like Saturday afternoon, when Franz and Emil come, doesn't she, Mr. Bhaer?" said Minnie.

"The 'effalunt' sat up, looking as much in earnest as any of them, and said soberly to me,—"I gif you my wort it is so, if we make too large a noise you shall say "Hush!" to us, and we go more softly."

CHAPTER 33: "JO'S JOURNAL"

There are a lot of different types of seed-cakes, from a whole loaf cake to something more like a cookie. This version makes cute little cakes that small imaginary lions would be happy to devour.

Makes about 12

- 1 tablespoon caraway seeds
- boiling water
- 8 ounces butter plus more for greasing the pans
- 8 ounces (1 cup) sugar
- 4 eggs
- 2 tablespoons brandy (optional)
- 8 ounces (2¼ cups) flour
- ½ teaspoon salt
- ½ teaspoon ground mace

1. Have all the ingredients at room temperature.

2. Preheat the oven to 350°F.

3. Put the caraway seeds in a small, heatproof dish and pour a few tablespoons of boiling water on them; let them sit while you mix the rest of the ingredients.

5. In the bowl of a stand mixer fitted with the paddle attachment, cream the butter and sugar together until light and fluffy.

6. Add the eggs and brandy, if using, and whip on high speed for 3 minutes until smooth and light.

7. In a medium bowl, mix the flour, salt, and mace together, then add to the egg mixture in four parts, mixing on medium speed until just combined.

8. Stir in the caraway seeds and any remaining liquid.

9. Portion the batter into greased muffin tins or other small cake pans, filling them three-quarters full.

10. Bake for 15 to 20 minutes, until a skewer inserted into the middle comes out clean.

CHAPTER 3

Beth

She was a housewifely little creature, and helped Hannah keep home neat and comfortable for the workers, never thinking of any reward but to be loved. Long, quiet days she spent, not lonely nor idle, for her little world was peopled with imaginary friends, and she was by nature a busy bee.

CHAPTER 4: "BURDENS"

Beth is like a warm, rosy lamp—a cozy presence that makes a house a home. When she's gone, the room feels suddenly cold and dark. We readers don't get to know Beth so much directly, but rather by seeing how she affects the people around her, particularly Jo. Beth is the only sister who doesn't get whole chapters in the book devoted to her personal experience, and she's so focused on the wants and needs of others that she reveals little about herself. But here are some endearing contradictions we observe about Beth: She considers herself stupid, but she has great talent and passion for music. She thinks she's unimportant, but her family relies on her for comfort and support. She's intensely shy, but she'll step up and reach out if someone needs her help. And she trusts only a small circle of loved ones, but there are a surprising number of people around town who regard her as the kindest of friends.

A domestic little being, Beth plays an active role in the March family food scene. While she's healthy, she goes marketing and helps Hannah around the kitchen daily, and we bet she makes little snacks for her sisters (especially for Jo when she's holed up in the attic writing). Beth's a girl of simple tastes; her favorite treat is fresh fruit. The dishes she likes best are humdrum yet heartening—perfect for eating by a crackling fire, wrapped up in quilts and surrounded by her sisters and parents: toast, for example, and the baked squash from the May 20 edition of *The Pickwick Portfolio*. When Beth is ill, she's offered more elaborate dishes, not because she wants fancy food, but because her family and friends need to channel all the love and fear and helplessness they're feeling into tangible gifts they can cook for her. This chapter includes recipes for Victorian remedies for the sick—some refreshing, others hearty and nourishing, and still others that are odd but worth a try.

The Beths of today would rather stay in for popcorn and board games than go out to the hipster gastropub. At a potluck, they are the ones who quietly remember to bring the plates and napkins everyone else forgot, instead of baking a showstopper cake to impress. Our Beths are cheerful bearers of emotional labor, who will make you macaroni and cheese and brownies if you're having a bad day, and show up with a thermos of chicken soup when you're under the weather. Comfort food is their specialty, although they get the most enjoyment out of giving it to others, rather than eating it themselves.

Toast for Tea

"I'll tell you what we'll do," said Beth; "let's each get her something for Christmas, and not get anything for ourselves."

"That's like you, dear! What will we get?" exclaimed Jo.

Every one thought soberly for a minute; then Meg announced, as if the idea was suggested by the sight of her own pretty hands, "I shall give her a nice pair of gloves."

"Army shoes, best to be had," cried Jo.

"Some handkerchiefs, all hemmed," said Beth.

"I'll get a little bottle of cologne; she likes it, and it won't cost much, so I'll have some left to buy my pencils," added Amy.

"How will we give the things?" asked Meg.

"Put them on the table, and bring her in and see her open the bundles. Don't you remember how we used to do on our birthdays?" answered Jo.

"I used to be *so* frightened when it was my turn to sit in the chair with the crown on, and see you all come marching round to give the presents, with a kiss. I liked the things and the kisses, but it was dreadful to have you sit looking at me while I opened the bundles," said Beth, who was toasting her face and the bread for tea at the same time.

CHAPTER I: "PLAYING PILGRIMS"

As the March household's little Vesta, Beth is in the habit of making everyone their late meal on the hearth. This toast that Beth might have prepared is a cheesy comfort food that's perfect for cold nights. Good Family Bread (page 142), is perfect for this, or another hearty bread.

Back before oven broilers, you would use something called a salamander to brown the top of a dish—it was sort of like a fireplace poker, but with a wide flat disk of iron at the bottom. You would heat the disk up in the fire till it was red hot, then hold it over whatever you wanted to cook. Clever!

Makes 4 servings

- 4 slices bread
- ¼ cup (½ stick) softened butter
- 1 teaspoon whole grain mustard
- 1½ cups shredded sharp cheddar cheese

1. Preheat the oven to 350°F. Toast your bread on the middle rack for 5 to 10 minutes, depending how brown you like it. You can put it on a baking sheet or put it straight on the rack. Flip halfway through.

2. Mix the butter and mustard together, and spread it on the toast. Sprinkle with grated cheese.

3. Turn on the oven's broiler and broil for 3 to 5 minutes, until the cheese is nicely toasted and browned.

Friendly Advice: Never walk away from the oven when you have something in the broiler, and check on it frequently, because everything will burn up if you're a minute too late!

Beth

"The History of a Squash"

Once upon a time a farmer planted a little seed in his garden, and after a while it sprouted and became a vine, and bore many squashes. One day in October, when they were ripe, he picked one and took it to market. A grocer-man bought and put it in his shop. That same morning, a little girl, in a brown hat and blue dress, with a round face and snub nose, went and bought it for her mother. She lugged it home, cut it up, and boiled it in the big pot; mashed some of it, with salt and butter, for dinner; and to the rest she added a pint of milk, two eggs, four spoons of sugar, nutmeg, and some crackers; put it in a deep dish, and baked it till it was brown and nice; and next day it was eaten by a family named March.

CHAPTER 10: "THE P.C. AND P.O."

The only actual recipe in the novel, Beth's story for *The Pickwick Portfolio* makes a light but cozy side dish. If you find the traditional Thanksgiving sweet potatoes with marshmallows to be overly sugary, this would make a nice alternative.

Makes 6 servings

- 2 pounds butternut squash, cut into 1-inch cubes
- 2 tablespoons salt
- 3 tablespoons butter, divided
- 2 cups whole milk

- 2 eggs
- 3 tablespoons brown sugar, divided
- ½ teaspoon nutmeg, plus a pinch more
- 30 crumbled saltine crackers (about 1½ cups crumbs), divided

1. Boil the squash with the salt in a large pot of water until soft, 15 to 20 minutes.

2. Drain the water and mash the squash with 2 tablespoons of the butter.

3. Preheat the oven to 375°F and butter a heatproof dish that holds at least 2 quarts.

4. Whisk the milk and eggs together in a medium bowl and add to the squash.

5. Add 2 tablespoons of the sugar, ½ teaspoon nutmeg, 1 cup cracker crumbs, and more salt if needed.

6. Melt the remaining 1 tablespoon butter, and mix in a small bowl with the remaining cracker crumbs, sugar, and nutmeg.

7. Put the squash in the prepared dish and sprinkle the top with the crumb mixture.

8. Bake until heated through and browned on top, 30 to 45 minutes. It should be puffed and slightly set in the middle.

Beth

Dainty Dishes

The pleasantest room in the house was set apart for Beth, and in it was gathered everything that she most loved,—flowers, pictures, her piano, the little work-table, and the beloved pussies. Father's best books found their way there, mother's easy-chair, Jo's desk, Amy's finest sketches; and every day Meg brought her babies on a loving pilgrimage, to make sunshine for Aunty Beth. John quietly set apart a little sum, that he might enjoy the pleasure of keeping the invalid supplied with the fruit she loved and longed for; old Hannah never wearied of concocting dainty dishes to tempt a capricious appetite, dropping tears as she worked; and from across the sea came little gifts and cheerful letters, seeming to bring breaths of warmth and fragrance from lands that know no winter.

CHAPTER 40: "THE VALLEY OF THE SHADOW"

Most Victorian cookbooks have a chapter on "invalid cookery," or food and remedies for the sick. In this era, home nursing was a woman's domain. In fact, female authority on the subject was a big reason why women were accepted as nurses in the Civil War, at a time when they might have been considered too weak to practice medicine.[6] Louisa May Alcott was a Civil War nurse herself![7]

Hannah, as an experienced cook and nurse, would have an arsenal of foods and beverages to combat illness. The novel doesn't specify what Hannah makes for her patients, other than boiled chicken and beef-tea, so we looked through historical books and picked out our favorite dainty dishes and drinks for you to try.

6   Veit, *Food in the Civil War Era*, 24.
7   Carolyn Strom Collins and Christina Wyss Eriksson, *Little Women Treasury* (New York: Viking Penguin, 1996), 8–9.

Beef-Tea

Mr. March told how he had longed to surprise them, and how, when the fine weather came, he had been allowed by his doctor to take advantage of it; how devoted Brooke had been, and how he was altogether a most estimable and upright young man. Why Mr. March paused a minute just there, and, after a glance at Meg, who was violently poking the fire, looked at his wife with an inquiring lift of the eyebrows, I leave you to imagine; also why Mrs. March gently nodded her head, and asked, rather abruptly, if he wouldn't have something to eat. Jo saw and understood the look; and she stalked grimly away to get wine and beef-tea, muttering to herself, as she slammed the door, "I hate estimable young men with brown eyes!"

CHAPTER 22: "PLEASANT MEADOWS"

This light beef broth is made with only meat, not bone, so it's clear instead of cloudy like today's bone broths. You can imagine it would be comforting if you were recovering from a long illness—food infusions like beef-tea, apple water, and toast water give you the illusion of eating when your stomach isn't quite ready for the real thing!

Makes 1 serving

- ½ pound lean beef stew meat
- 1½ cups boiling water
- salt

1. Cut off any fat and chop the beef into 1-inch pieces. Sprinkle with salt.

2. Heat a frying pan very hot (no oil) and quickly brown the meat on all sides.

3. Transfer to a small saucepan and pour boiling water over it, then heat on low (not boiling) for 30 minutes.

4. Strain into a mug and add salt if desired (and if allowed by medical advice).

Modest Chicken

Two easy-chairs stood side by side at the head of the table, in which sat Beth and her father, feasting modestly on chicken and a little fruit.

CHAPTER 22: "PLEASANT MEADOWS"

You might think boiled chicken would be tasteless, but as long as you don't overcook it, it will come out moist and tender, and it's much less messy than roasting it—the only trade-off is that you don't get the crispy skin. It's very nice with drawn butter (page 89). If you like liver, it can be cooked, mashed, and added to the drawn butter sauce.

Makes 2 or 3 servings

- 1 whole chicken
- water
- 2 tablespoons salt

1. Fill a large stockpot with enough water to cover the chicken and add salt. Set it to boil over high heat.

2. Remove the neck and giblets from the cavity of the chicken (save them for broth if you like, or just toss them).

3. When the water boils, put in the chicken and return to a boil. Turn down the heat to medium-low and simmer, covered, for 45 minutes.

4. Remove from heat and let stand until the internal temperature of the chicken has reached 165°F.

5. Take the chicken out and divide it into bone-in pieces or remove all the meat from the bones, depending how you'd like to serve it. It can be served warm with a drawn butter sauce or cold in sandwiches or chicken salad.

Friendly Advice: The cooking water can be saved to make broth—after you remove the meat, put the bones, giblets (except the liver), and neck back in the water. Add onion, carrot, and celery, and simmer uncovered until the flavors are concentrated to your taste.

Beth

Vegetable Soup

Nourishing and surprisingly full-flavored, this soup is wonderful paired with a slice of crusty bread. The rice and flour thicken the broth so that it feels much richer than it is.

Makes 4 servings

- 2 turnips, peeled and diced
- 2 carrots, peeled and diced
- 4 potatoes, peeled and diced
- 1 large onion, diced
- 1 parsnip, peeled and diced
- 2 to 3 stalks celery, diced
- 1 tablespoon long-grain rice
- 12 cups (3 quarts) water
- 2 tablespoons butter
- 2 tablespoons flour

1. Put the turnips, carrots, potatoes, onion, parsnip, and celery in a large pot, along with the water and rice.

2. Bring to a boil over medium-high heat, and then lower to keep it at a steady, gentle boil for 3 hours. Stir occasionally to keep the vegetables from sticking to the bottom.

3. Strain the soup through a colander and put the vegetable broth back in the pot over medium heat.

4. Add the butter and stir until melted.

5. Put the flour in a small bowl, and then add just enough broth to whisk it into a paste. Mix in another ladleful of soup to it, and then repeat. Then, add to the pot and stir. (If you just put flour directly in the soup, it'll turn into little balls of flour on the surface without dissolving.)

6. Bring to a boil, and then serve.

Friendly Advice: You can discard the cooked vegetables after Step 3, but if you can't bear to waste that much food, they aren't bad when mashed together with plenty of milk, butter, salt, and pepper.

Tidbit of History: Deeply Misguided Victorian Remedies

A lot of the remedies in Victorian cookbooks might be helpful and comforting, but others sound downright disgusting or are flat-out dangerous. Check out these poor choices! And in case it's not obvious—don't try these at home.

❧⚬❀⚬❧

An ointment made from the common ground-worms, which boys dig to bait fishes, rubbed on with the hand, is said to be excellent, when the sinews are drawn up by any disease or accident.

We don't understand how this could possibly help your sinews.

❧⚬❀⚬❧

For a prick with a pin, or a slight cut, nothing will more effectually stop the bleeding than old cobwebs compressed into a lump and applied to the wound, or bound on it with a rag. A scrap of cotton wadding is also good for stopping blood.

Old cobwebs don't sound very hygienic, even if you don't have gauze around.

❧⚬❀⚬❧

Break a fresh egg into a saucer, and mix a little sugar with it; also, if approved, a small quantity of wine. Beat the whole to a strong froth. It is considered a restorative.

Even if you're not worried about risking salmonella, is it possible to drink a raw-egg-and-wine cocktail without vomiting?

❧⚬❀⚬❧

And here's the doozy: *Mix two table-spoonfuls of extract of lead with a bottle of rain or river water. Then add two table-spoonfuls of brandy, and shake it well.* The cookbook even confidently adds the footnote: *These remedies are all very simple; but the author knows them to have been efficacious whenever tried.*

Yeah, no. We think it goes without saying that no one should ever drink lead.

Beth

Hot Lemonade

One of the more appealing home remedies of the time period, we imagine Victorians drinking this like we do Emergen-C. It's pleasant, fragrant, and, in its original form, intensely sweet—the original recipe calls for half a cup of sugar! Unless you're trying to soothe a cough, we don't suggest using that much. Either way, it's excellent with a splash of brandy. Don't worry, even the Marches approved of medicinal alcohol.

Makes 4 servings

- 1 lemon
- 2 tablespoons sugar, or to taste
- 4 cups (1 quart) boiling water
- brandy (optional)

1. Slice the lemon, leaving the rind on.

2. In a large, heatproof bowl, mix the sugar into the lemon, using a spoon, until it becomes pasty. Smash the lemon a little to better release the juice.

3. Pour the boiling water into the mixture and stir until the sugar dissolves. Add brandy to taste, if using.

4. Serve in teacups.

Toast Water

Makes 2 servings

- 2 slices bread
- 4 cups (1 quart) water

1. Toast the bread until it's browned but not at all burnt on both sides (dry, no butter) and boil the water.

2. Put the toast in a heatproof bowl and pour the boiling water over it.

3. Let stand until it is cool, then drain out the water into a pitcher. Don't squeeze the bread too much or you'll get crumbs.

4. Discard the mushy bread and serve the toast water chilled.

Apple Water

Makes 2 servings

- 4 cups (1 quart) boiling water
- 2 tart apples, like Granny Smith
- zest of 1 lemon
- ½ tablespoon sugar, or to taste (optional)

1. While the water is boiling, thinly slice the apples (no need to remove skin or core) and place in a large bowl with the lemon zest and sugar, if using.

2. Pour the boiling water over the apples, cover, and let stand until cool.

3. Strain the liquid from of the apples and serve the apple water chilled.

4. Discard the apples or save for another use, like applesauce or apple pancakes.

Beth

CHAPTER 4

Amy

Amy, though the youngest, was a most important person,—in her own opinion at least. A regular snow-maiden, with blue eyes, and yellow hair curling on her shoulders, pale and slender, and always carrying herself like a young lady mindful of her manners.

CHAPTER I: "PLAYING PILGRIMS"

Amy gets a bad rap. Let this book to be the first to tell you: You don't have to be anti-Amy to be Team Jo. In fact, if you love Jo, you can find plenty to appreciate in the most maligned of March sisters.

When *Little Women* fans and scholars trash poor Amy, they're often talking about who she is as a 12-year-old. Yes, she burns Jo's manuscript, which is egregious, and we might even go so far as to say that Amy deserves that ice-water dunk. But no one should be judged for what they did as a preteen, and Amy has one of the most compelling character arcs in the story, going from the annoying family baby to a practical yet high-minded woman who ends up marrying for love.

Grown-up Amy is the popular girl who always knows what to say and wear, and whose hair is somehow flawless all the time. Not very relatable at first glance, maybe. But we also witness how she *works* to achieve this image. She can't afford to go out and order the latest couture from Parisian fashion houses. Amy paints old boots and hats to make them look like new satin, and she accents a hand-me-down dress with tulle for a ball where she wants to look particularly pretty. Let's not forget too that Amy is a creative and ambitious artist with a burning desire to see the world and prove herself. Her best chance at getting out of her parents' house and going abroad is to make the right connections in society. She knows her own strengths, and as a woman of modest means, she's working to use them to her advantage in a world built for wealthy men.

When it comes to eating and drinking, Amy likes the trendy, the sweet, and the fancy. If Amy were a millennial foodie, she would be angling to snag an invite to that molecular gastronomy bistro that just opened downtown. She might consider the plating and presentation of a dish more important than the taste. She would always want an overly intricate dessert. And she'd have a killer Instagram account documenting restaurant visits with her social media influencer friends.

In this chapter, we return to the Victorian era and present some of Amy's favorite treats from the book. In the story, Amy uses food to indulge or impress, and so can you. Here we have the tempting pickled limes that she needed to win status among her schoolmates. There's jelly for her sweet tooth. You can also attend the elegant lunch she organizes for snooty fellow art students, and if you're feeling really ambitious, sample a Christmas ball menu from her stay in a hotel in Nice, France.

Lovely Pickled Limes

Next day Amy was rather late at school; but could not resist the temptation of displaying, with pardonable pride, a moist brown-paper parcel, before she consigned it to the inmost recesses of her desk. During the next few minutes the rumor that Amy March had got twenty-four delicious limes (she ate one on the way), and was going to treat circulated through her "set," and the attentions of her friends became quite overwhelming.

CHAPTER 7:
"AMY'S VALLEY OF HUMILIATION"

Pickled limes are probably the most iconic food item in *Little Women*, but most people nowadays don't have any idea what they are like. You might imagine something marmalade-like and sweet, but in fact they are very bitter and rather salty—similar to the preserved citrus pickles that are still common in Middle Eastern, Indian, and Southeast Asian cooking today. The question is, why would school-age children have been so enamored of them? Think of it as an early equivalent of Atomic Fireballs, Warheads, Flamin' Hot Cheetos, etc.—kids seem to like challenging themselves and each other with super-intense snack foods. Not to mention, they were cheap because they were sent over from India in big barrels filled with seawater. Not much processing required!

If you don't want to just eat them furtively out of your desk, you can slice the limes thinly and muddle them with sugar in a glass of seltzer. It'll have a bitter twist, like tonic water.

Makes 1 dozen

- 2 ounces salt
- 4 cups water
- 12 small Mexican or Key limes

1. Dissolve the salt in the water (this was often described as "brine that will bear an egg" because there's enough salt to make an egg float).

2. Wash the limes well and put them in a jar(s) with a lid. Add as much brine as will fill the jar, with about ½ inch of space at the top.

3. Close the jar and leave it in a cool cabinet for about five months (to approximate the sea voyage from India), turning it over every so often to slosh the brine around. Eventually, the peels will turn tender and translucent, and fade to an olive-green color.

4. If you're in a hurry, instead of the five-month cure you can put the jar, lid on loosely, in a very low oven (200°F) for 6 to 8 hours to accelerate the process.

5. At this point, the limes should be similar to what Amy had at school. The bitter citrus taste isn't exactly pleasant, but it certainly wakes up your mouth!

In Another Pickle

We are fairly sure that the above method is the type of lime that Amy would have bought for a penny in a shop, but home cooks had another method for pickling limes as follows: Cut a deep cross into the bottom of each lime and pack it with salt. Put the limes into a jar with a bit more salt and leave it to stand on the counter for a week, shaking it once a day. At the end of the week, drain off any brine and rinse off the salt. Replace the limes in the jar and cover with hot white vinegar that you have boiled with a variety of whole spices, such as mustard seeds, cloves, black peppercorns, fresh ginger, dried chiles, or garlic. Add the spices to the jar as well, and let them continue to pickle for up to a year, or use the oven method above. This makes a pickle that's less bitter, but much more salty and sour. You can mince the limes and add them sparingly to sauces and dressings, or as an accompaniment to hearty dishes like Mathematical Mutton Curry (page 28). The flavor will be intense and exciting—a little goes a long way! The preserving liquid can also be used—one recipe calls it a "lemon catsup."

Apple Jelly

Ma Chere Mamma,—

We are all well I do my lessons always and never corroberate the girls—Meg says I mean contradick so I put in both words and you can take the properest. Meg is a great comfort to me and lets me have jelly every night at tea its so good for me Jo says because it keeps me sweet tempered.

CHAPTER 16: "CHAPTER LETTERS"

You don't have to use pink apples here, but they make a gorgeous blush-colored jelly that would suit Amy's refined taste perfectly.

A jelly bag is nice to have for this—it's a muslin bag that hangs on a stand over a bowl, allowing the juice to drain out slowly without any pulp getting through. You can rig up a makeshift version by lining a colander with several layers of cheesecloth and setting it over a bowl.

Makes about 1 pint

- 3 large, tart pink apples, like Cameo, Gala, Pink Lady
- juice of 1 lemon
- about 1 pound white sugar (about 1¾ cups)

1. Wash the apples well and cut them in eighths. Do not peel or core them.

2. Put the apples in a medium saucepan with enough water to just cover.

3. Boil over high heat with the lid on until they are soft enough to easily mash with the back of a spoon, about 30 minutes.

4. Transfer the juice and pulp to a jelly bag, set over a bowl. Let drain for a few hours or overnight. The juice may still be cloudy at this point, but don't worry.

5. When you're ready to start cooking, put a small plate in the freezer.

6. Add the lemon juice to the drained apple juice, and weigh it. Combine with an equal weight of sugar in a medium saucepan.

7. Boil over high heat until foam appears on top. Skim off the foam and you will see the liquid is now clear.

8. Reduce the heat to low and simmer for 5 to 10 minutes, stirring often, until you can see it starting to thicken a bit when you let it run off the spoon, or until it reaches 220°F on a candy thermometer (an instant-read or laser thermometer doesn't work well for this).

9. Test it by dropping a small spoonful on the cold plate and putting it back in the freezer for 1 minute. Take it out again and push your finger through the jelly on the plate. If it wrinkles as you push it, it's done. If not, keep boiling and try again in a few minutes.

10. Once it's finished, transfer to jars and refrigerate or process for canning.

Friendly Advice: It's easy to scale this recipe to any amount of fruit—just weigh your juice after it's drained and use the same weight of sugar.

Amy's
Little
Artistic Fête

"Our drawing class breaks up next week, and before the girls separate for the summer, I want to ask them out here for a day. They are wild to see the river, sketch the broken bridge, and copy some of the things they admire in my book. They have been very kind to me in many ways, and I am grateful, for they are all rich, and I know I am poor, yet they never made any difference."

"Why should they?" and Mrs. March put the question with what the girls called her "Maria Theresa air."

"You know as well as I that it *does* make a difference with nearly every one, so don't ruffle up, like a dear, motherly hen, when your chickens get pecked by smarter birds; the ugly duckling turned out a swan, you know;" and Amy smiled without bitterness, for she possessed a happy temper and hopeful spirit.

Mrs. March laughed, and smoothed down her maternal pride as she asked,—

"Well, my swan, what is your plan?"

"I should like to ask the girls out to lunch next week, to take them [for] a drive to the places they want to see, a row on the river, perhaps, and make a little artistic *fête* for them."

"That looks feasible. What do you want for lunch? Cake, sandwiches, fruit, and coffee will be all that is necessary, I suppose?"

"Oh dear, no! We must have cold tongue and chicken, French chocolate and ice-cream, besides. The girls are used to such things, and I want my lunch to be proper and elegant, though I *do* work for my living."

Chapter 26: "Artistic Attempts"

Oof, we feel bad for Amy in this episode. She wants so badly to fit in with her wealthier art classmates, even while feeling the stinging differences between what she and they can afford. Amy and her family go to huge lengths to offer an afternoon's entertainment that might be considered acceptable by this snootier crowd, and after all that trouble, only one person shows up out of the expected 12! The humiliation! It's a teenager's worst nightmare—the popular friends you're trying to win over don't even bother showing up at the party you threw for them. Poor Amy! But the menu selections for this luncheon are certainly elegant and delicious, so soothe your secondhand embarrassment with some of Amy's favorite delicate fare.

Proper Roast Chicken

This roast chicken, dredged in flour and basted multiple times in butter, has a rich, crispy crust. The chicken is served with a sauce called drawn butter (not just melted butter as we think of it today). It's one of those recipes that sound bizarre at first but turn out to be surprisingly good.

Makes 3 to 4 servings

- 1 whole roasting chicken, skin on, about 4 pounds
- 1½ teaspoons sea salt
- 2 teaspoons pepper, plus about 1 teaspoon more for the butter
- 6 tablespoons (¾ stick) butter, divided
- ⅓ cup flour, sifted
- drawn butter (recipe on page 89)

1. Preheat the oven to 375°F.

2. Sprinkle the chicken all over, inside and out, with the salt and pepper, rubbing it into the skin.

3. Take 2 tablespoons of butter, coat it in about 1 teaspoon of pepper, and put it in the chicken cavity.

4. Dredge the chicken in the flour, shaking off any extra.

5. Melt the remaining 4 tablespoons butter. Use it to butter the roasting pan a little, then baste the chicken all over with a basting brush.

6. Place the chicken in the pan, breast-up, and put it in the oven.

7. Have the melted butter on hand. Every 20 minutes, take out the chicken, close the oven door, and baste the meat all over with melted butter. Return the chicken to the oven as quickly as possible.

8. Roast 20 minutes for every pound of chicken. Check the internal temperature after an hour of roasting by inserting a meat thermometer through the thickest part of the thigh, avoiding the bone, and check the temperature gauge after 10 seconds. The internal temperature of the thigh should be 165°F.

9. Let the chicken rest for 10 minutes while you make the drawn butter sauce.

10. Carve and serve.

Drawn Butter

Makes 1 cup

- ½ cup whole milk
- ½ cup (1 stick) softened butter
- ½ tablespoon minced fresh parsley
- ½ tablespoon flour

1. Heat the milk in a small saucepan over medium-low heat until just starting to bubble.

2. In a small bowl, mash together the butter, parsley, and flour.

3. Pour the milk over the butter and stir quickly to combine.

4. Return the mixture to the saucepan and bring to a boil over medium heat, stirring constantly, until it starts to foam up.

5. Immediately remove it from the heat and transfer to a warmed serving bowl or gravy boat.

Cold Tongue Sandwiches

If you've never tried tongue before, don't be scared! Prepared this way, it tastes very similar to corned beef. The texture is a little more rubbery than other cuts of beef, but sliced thin it's very tasty.

The French rolls are an interesting recipe; we're not quite sure what the reasoning was for adding the whipped egg whites in this way, but the result is a fine, light bread that makes cute little sandwiches. The method here doesn't seem especially French, but young Amy's French is always an approximation anyway ...

Makes 9 small sandwiches

For cold tongue:

- 8 cups (2 quarts) water
- 1½ cups salt
- 2 tablespoons pink curing salt
- ½ cup molasses
- 1 beef tongue, 3 to 4 pounds
- 4 cups ice
- 2 bay leaves
- 1 teaspoon peppercorns

For 9 small French rolls:

- 2 tablespoons butter
- 1 cup milk
- 1 pound flour (about 4 cups)
- 1 tablespoon salt
- 1 tablespoon sugar
- 1 packet active dry or instant yeast (2¼ teaspoons)
- 3 egg whites
- vegetable oil, for greasing

For the sandwiches:

- butter, softened
- parsley sprigs, for garnish

PREPARE THE COLD TONGUE:

1. Start at least 10 days before you want to eat. Combine the water, salt, pink curing salt, and molasses in a large stock pot that will hold the tongue and will fit in your refrigerator. Heat on high until the salt and molasses are dissolved, then remove from heat and allow to cool.

2. Rinse off the tongue and trim off some of the gristly part at the back if you like.

3. Add the ice to the brine in the pot, and stir until the mixture is completely cold.

4. Put the tongue in the pot, making sure it's completely submerged. If it floats, place a ceramic bowl or other heavy nonreactive object on top to keep it under the brine.

5. Put the whole contraption in the refrigerator and leave it for 10 days. Check on it every day or so and flip the meat over so it brines evenly.

WHEN YOU ARE READY TO COOK THE TONGUE:

1. Pour off the brine and rinse the tongue well. Wash the pot.

2. Return the meat to the pot and fill it with enough water to cover the meat by an inch or so. Add the bay leaves and peppercorns.

3. Simmer over low heat so it's barely bubbling for about 3 hours, until tender, or 150°F in the center. Check it occasionally and add more water as needed.

4. Drain the tongue and allow it to cool for a bit.

5. Peel the skin off the tongue—it should pull off easily. (This is probably the creepiest part of the process, our apologies.)

6. Slice the tongue thinly and serve in sandwiches or however you like. You'll find that the part toward the root of the tongue is fattier and more tender.

Amy

PREPARE THE ROLLS:

1. Put the butter and milk in a small saucepan over medium heat and warm until the butter is mostly melted. Don't let it get too hot; you should be able to put your finger in without burning yourself.

2. While the milk is warming, combine the flour, salt, sugar, and yeast in a large bowl.

3. Add the milk and butter to the flour mixture and stir well.

4. In a medium bowl, beat the egg whites to soft peaks and fold them into the dough. It may seem too dry at first, but it will soften up.

5. Knead the dough by hand or in a stand mixer until it feels silky and not too sticky. You should be able to stretch an edge of the dough until it's translucent without tearing (this is called the "windowpane test"). As you knead, add a little additional flour as needed, but not so much that the dough becomes stiff.

6. Oil the bowl you were using (no need to wash it) and put the dough in, turning it to coat.

7. Cover and let rise for about 1 hour in a warm place.

8. Generously grease a 9 x 9-inch baking pan with vegetable oil.

9. Once the dough has grown puffy (if you poke it, it should not spring back) and has nearly doubled in size, gently punch down the dough.

10. Divide the dough into 9 equal pieces, and form each piece into a tight ball (smooth on top and tucked in tightly underneath). Pour a little oil in your hands and gently roll each ball in your hands to coat it with a light layer of oil.

11. Place the rolls close together in the baking pan, spacing them evenly. Cover with oiled plastic wrap and let rise in a warm place for about 1 hour, or until doubled in size. They will be touching on all sides.

12. While the rolls are rising, preheat the oven to 375°F.

13. Bake the rolls for 20 to 25 minutes, until the tops are golden brown and the internal temperature is about 200°F for the outer rolls and 180°F or so for the middle (they will keep cooking a bit after you take them out).

14. Let the rolls cool for 5 to 10 minutes in the pan, then remove and separate them.

PREPARE THE SANDWICHES:

1. Split some French rolls and butter them.

2. Lay a generous amount of cold tongue slices on the lower half of the bread. If you want to make more space for filling, you can scoop out a little of the inside of the top half.

3. Press the two halves of the bread together.

4. Pile the sandwiches in a pyramid on a flat dish, and garnish with sprigs of fresh parsley.

Friendly Advice: Tongue was often smoked after curing, to further preserve it. Period recipes say to smoke it for several weeks(!) but since we don't need to worry so much about preservation, we tried smoking it after boiling, at 225°F for 2 to 3 hours, which made a great variation!

Get the Receipt

If you want an example of a vague historical recipe, look no further than the original 19th-century receipt for French rolls from Eliza Leslie's *Directions for Cookery, In Its Various Branches* (1840):

> Sift a pound of flour into a pan, and rub into it two ounces of butter; mix in the whites only of three eggs, beaten to a stiff froth, and a table-spoonful of strong yeast; add sufficient milk to make a stiff dough, and a salt-spoonful of salt. Cover it and set it before the fire to rise. It should be light in an hour. Then put it on a paste-board, divide it into rolls, or round cakes; lay them in a floured square pan, and bake them about ten minutes in a quick oven.

Amy

Delicious Cake

White Mountain frosting, also called boiled icing or Italian meringue, is a beautiful, glossy, pure-white frosting with a marshmallowy texture. Combined with a delicate vanilla cake, it was one of the first true layer cakes, and would have been just the thing for an aesthetically minded young lady with a sweet tooth to serve at her "artistic fête."

Makes 8 servings

For the cake:
- ½ cup (1 stick) butter
- 1 cup sugar
- 2 whole eggs plus 1 egg yolk
- 1¾ cups flour
- ½ cup buttermilk
- ½ tablespoon vanilla extract
- ½ teaspoon baking soda
- ¼ teaspoon salt

For the frosting:
- 3 egg whites, at room temperature
- 2 cups sugar
- ½ teaspoon cream of tartar
- ⅓ cup water
- 1 teaspoon vanilla extract
- tiny pinch of salt

PREPARE THE CAKE:

1. Have all the ingredients at room temperature.

2. Preheat the oven to 350°F. Butter 2 (8-inch) cake pans and dust them with flour.

3. In the bowl of a stand mixer using the paddle attachment, cream the butter and sugar together on high speed for 3 to 5 minutes, until light and fluffy.

4. Add the whole eggs and egg yolk. Whip on high speed until very smooth. If it looks curdled, keep whipping.

5. Add half the flour, mix, then add the buttermilk and vanilla, mix, then add the rest of the flour along with the baking soda and salt.

6. Divide the batter evenly into the cake pans.

7. Bake about 20 minutes (this can vary a lot depending on your oven; start checking at 15 minutes), until a skewer inserted in the center of one cake comes out clean.

8. Let the cakes cool in the pans for 15 minutes, then remove them from the pans and let them finish cooling completely before frosting.

PREPARE THE FROSTING:

1. Wait until the cakes are completely cooled to start making the frosting, because you need to spread it on the cake while the frosting is still warm.

2. Whip the egg whites to stiff peaks in a metal bowl and set aside.

3. Combine the sugar, cream of tartar, and water in a small saucepan over medium heat and stir gently until it comes to a boil. Clip a candy thermometer to the side of the pan. Wash down the sides of the saucepan with a wet pastry brush and continue to boil, without stirring, until it reaches the soft ball stage (235°F to 240°F).

9. Spread frosting between the cake layers and all over the outside in snowy peaks. It works best to pile the frosting on top and sort of coax it down the sides—you need to work quickly while the frosting is still warm. Once it cools, it sets up and becomes very, very sticky.

4. Pour the sugar syrup into the egg whites in a thin stream, whipping constantly at medium speed until incorporated. Try not to pour the sugar syrup directly on the beater or on the sides of the bowl.

5. Mix in the vanilla and salt and whip on high speed until stiff peaks form, 1 to 2 minutes.

6. Immediately spread the frosting on the cake before it sets up!

Elegant Raspberry Ice Cream

In New England, strawberries are in season from May to June, and raspberries from June to September. Amy's fête takes place in midsummer, so raspberry ice cream it is! Its charming pink color would be elegant enough even for Amy's fancy girlfriends.

Makes 4 to 6 servings

- 12 ounces raspberries (frozen are fine, but thaw them first)
- 1 tablespoon lemon juice
- ½ cup sugar
- pinch of salt
- 1 cup whole milk
- 1 cup heavy cream
- 2 tablespoons corn syrup

1. Combine the raspberries, lemon juice, sugar, and salt in a large bowl and mash them together until juicy.

2. Whisk in the milk and cream.

3. Put a fine strainer over another bowl and pour the mixture through, using a spoon to squeeze out as much of the raspberry pulp as you can. You should be left with a bunch of seeds in the strainer.

4. Whisk the corn syrup into the raspberry cream.

5. Churn in an ice cream maker (hand crank for authenticity, or electric for convenience), then serve right away. If you need to store the ice cream in the freezer before serving, let it warm up a bit before scooping—it can get a bit icy.

French Chocolate

This is just a fancy version of hot cocoa! Solid chocolate in bar form would have been a fairly new product at this time, and milk chocolate wasn't invented until 1875; the type of chocolate they did have apparently required a long time boiling in water in order to extract the flavor. They would then add milk or cream, and sugar to taste, much like coffee.

Makes 2 servings

- 2 cups whole milk
- 2 ounces semisweet chocolate, chopped
- tiny pinch of salt
- ¼ teaspoon freshly grated nutmeg (optional)

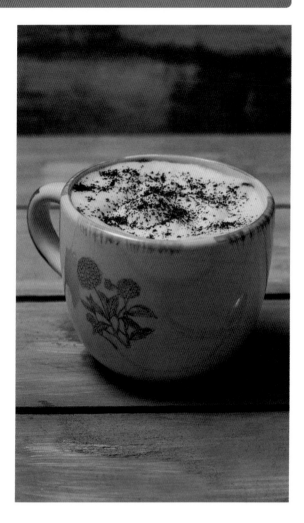

1. Warm the milk in a small saucepan over low heat just until it starts to bubble around the edges.

2. Add the chocolate, salt, and nutmeg, if using, and stir until the chocolate is melted.

3. Using a whisk (or a hand mixer or stick blender, if you want to be modern), whip the chocolate till frothy.

4. Serve in small cups, with the foam on top.

Christmas
Ball Supper
in Nice

The company assembled in the long *salle à manger*, that evening, was such as one sees nowhere but on the Continent. The hospitable Americans had invited every acquaintance they had in Nice, and, having no prejudice against titles, secured a few to add luster to their Christmas ball. [...]

It was a lively scene, for soon the spirit of the social season took possession of every one, and Christmas merriment made all faces shine, hearts happy, and heels light. The musicians fiddled, tooted, and banged as if they enjoyed it; everybody danced who could, and those who couldn't admired their neighbors with uncommon warmth. The air was dark with Davises, and many Joneses gambolled like a flock of young giraffes. The golden secretary darted through the room like a meteor, with a dashing Frenchwoman, who carpeted the floor with her pink satin train. The Serene Teuton found the supper-table, and was happy, eating steadily through the bill of fare, and dismayed the *garcons* by the ravages he committed.

CHAPTER 37: "NEW IMPRESSIONS"

Amy's social grace and talent for art are rewarded by an extended tour of Europe with wealthy relations. While she's in Nice, she reunites with Laurie, who's still miserable from Jo's rejection. They attend a Christmas ball together, where they both see each other with new eyes—it's the beginning of their romance.

In the March sisters' world, French cuisine is revered as the highest and most distinguished of all. If you're up for a challenge, try your hand at Amy and Laurie's Christmas supper in Nice! Since the novel doesn't spell out what they eat, we scoured menus from the 1800s to find out what a fancy French party might have served back then. A heads-up: These dishes are pretty complicated to prepare, so it would be extremely helpful to have a few days and several kitchen minions to devote to the task.

Quenelles de Volaille au Consommé (Consommé with Chicken Dumplings)

A clear consommé is the most elevated form of stock in French cuisine—a staple one must master to work in the kitchens. Consommé is listed as the first course on many a menu for a grand French supper. Try it with these hearty chicken dumplings.

Makes 5 or 6 servings

For the chicken consommé:

- 1 onion
- 4 whole cloves
- 2 bay leaves
- 1½ pounds boneless, skinless chicken breast and thigh
- 2 carrots, peeled and julienned
- 6 egg whites
- 3 quarts strong chicken stock, cold and strained through mesh
- 3 sprigs parsley
- 2 sprigs thyme

For the quenelles:

- 6 cups fresh bread crumbs
- 1 scant cup milk
- 1 cup butter
- ¼ teaspoon salt
- ½ teaspoon pepper
- pinch of freshly grated nutmeg
- ½ pound uncooked chicken breast, diced
- 1 egg, beaten and strained through a sieve
- handful of salt, for boiling
- sautéed seasonal vegetables, for serving (optional)

PREPARE THE CHICKEN CONSOMMÉ:

1. Make two onions pique: Peel the onion and cut it in half horizontally. Put each half rings-side down on a cutting board or plate, and use 2 cloves for each like pushpins to fasten a bay leaf to the top.

2. On a dry cast-iron skillet, put the onions, rings-side down, on high heat for 5 to 7 minutes until blackened.

3. Cube the chicken breast. Put it in a food processor in batches until it's as small as possible. Add the carrots and process some more.

4. In a separate medium bowl, whisk the egg whites for 30 seconds. Add the ground chicken and carrots. Thoroughly mix by hand until it forms a paste.

5. Place the onions pique in the bottom of a large pot, and then the meat mixture. Cover with the cold stock. Make a *bouquet garni* by tying the sprigs of parsley and thyme together with cooking twine, and add it to the pot.

6. Set the pot over high heat. Stir constantly as it heats up for 15 minutes or until the temperature hits 120°F. Lower the heat to a simmer.

7. A floating raft of the processed chicken, vegetables, and egg whites will form. Push a ladle into the center of the raft to make a small hole. Gently simmer for 45 to 60 minutes, basting every 5 minutes. (To baste, scoop up a ladleful of broth from the center and pour it in a circle over the raft.)

8. Strain through a mesh sieve covered in fine cheesecloth.

PREPARE THE QUENELLES:

1. Put the bread crumbs in milk and let soak for 10 minutes.

2. In a medium saucepan over medium heat, cook the soaked bread crumbs for 2 to 3 minutes, mixing vigorously with a wooden spoon, until they form a sticky ball of dough.

3. Let the dough cool, and then stir in the softened butter. Season with salt, pepper, and nutmeg.

4. Add the diced chicken to the bread crumb mixture.

5. Process the meat and bread crumbs in a food processor until smooth. Add the egg and process until incorporated.

6. Put a large pot of water with the handful of salt over high heat until it boils, then lower the heat to medium-high.

7. Shape about 2 tablespoons of dough into an oval with 2 large tablespoons and drop into the salted water. Repeat with the remaining dough, until you have enough for one layer floating in the pot. Poach over medium-high heat for 10 minutes, turning the quenelles over halfway through. Repeat until all the dough is cooked.

8. Drain the quenelles of excess water and put in a bowl, along with sautéed seasonal vegetables.

9. Ladle in warm consommé and serve immediately.

Friendly Advice: Two traditional French techniques in this recipe might be unfamiliar. An *oignon piqué*, or onion pique, is where a chef uses whole cloves like pushpins to attach a bay leaf (or leaves) to an onion. This method makes it easier to take all of them out at once before serving. A *bouquet garni* is a bundle of herbs, usually tied together with cooking twine or placed in a cheesecloth bag. Both the *oignon piqué* and *bouquet garni* can add flavor to soups, stews, and sauces.

Saumons au Beurre de Montpellier (Salmon with Montpellier Butter)

"Montpellier butter" at this time was more like a mayonnaise and did not contain any actual butter. Nowadays people seem to have taken the name more literally and it's usually served as a compound butter, flavored with many of the same herbs, anchovies, pickles, etc., but our version is the classic non-butter style.

Makes 4 servings

For the poached salmon:

- 1 tablespoon butter
- 1 medium onion, sliced
- 2 carrots
- 1 bay leaf
- 4 or 5 sprigs fresh thyme
- 1 clove garlic, minced
- 1 tablespoon minced fresh ginger
- 1 whole clove
- 1 cup white wine
- 1 teaspoon salt
- 1 large salmon fillet, about 2 pounds
- butter lettuce leaves
- boiled egg white, truffles, anchovy fillets, capers, crayfish tails, and aspic jelly croutons, for garnishing (optional)

For the Montpellier butter:

- yolks of 3 hard-boiled eggs
- 1 tablespoon watercress
- 1 tablespoon tarragon
- 2 or 3 spinach leaves for color
- 1 teaspoon capers
- 4 cornichon pickles
- 2 anchovies
- 1 raw egg yolk
- 1 cup mild olive oil
- 1 tablespoon white vinegar
- 2 teaspoons Dijon mustard
- 1 teaspoon pepper
- 1 teaspoon salt

Amy

PREPARE THE POACHED SALMON:

1. In a large fish poacher, melt the butter over medium heat and sauté the onion, carrots, bay leaf, thyme, garlic, ginger, and clove until they've browned, 5 to 10 minutes.

2. Add the wine and salt, and bring to a boil, then reduce the heat and simmer for 8 minutes. (This is called a *court-bouillon*.)

3. Add the salmon and poach for 8 to 10 minutes, or just until cooked.

4. Let it cool in the juices.

5. Drain and remove the skin if there is any.

6. Put the salmon on a serving platter lined with lettuce leaves.

7. Spread the salmon with a layer of Montpellier butter.

8. Decorate with whatever garnishes you like.

PREPARE THE MONTPELLIER BUTTER:

1. In a food processor, combine the boiled egg yolks, watercress, tarragon, spinach, capers, pickles, and anchovies. Process till it forms a paste.

2. Add the raw egg yolk and process some more.

3. Slowly add olive oil in a thin stream while processing. Stop and scrape the sides periodically, to make sure each bit of olive oil is fully incorporated before adding more.

4. Add vinegar, mustard, pepper, and salt, and process to combine.

5. If you want an extra-smooth sauce, pass it through a cheesecloth or fine sieve.

Fonds d'Artichauts à l'Italienne (Italian-Style Artichoke Hearts)

French cooking is all about sauces, and sauces within sauces! It makes sense to use the simpler sauces as building blocks for more complex ones; that is, if you have a kitchen full of apprentices whose job it is to make vats of each sauce every morning.

Makes 4 servings

- juice of 1 lemon or ¼ cup vinegar
- 8 small artichokes
- Italian sauce (recipe follows)
- salt

1. Fill a large pot with water and the lemon juice or vinegar.

2. Trim the artichokes, dipping them in the lemon water a few times during the process, to keep them from turning brown. Leave the finished ones in the water while you do the others.

3. To trim the artichokes, pull off the outer leaves until you get to the tender yellow inner ones.

4. Slice the top inch off with a serrated knife, then cut them in half and scoop out the choke.

5. Once you've got them all trimmed, drain the lemon water and refill the pot with clean water and several tablespoons of salt. Add the artichokes and boil until tender, 15 to 20 minutes.

6. Drain the artichokes and combine with the Italian sauce, and allow to marinate an hour or so before serving at room temperature. Season with salt to taste.

Friendly Advice: It's a big help to look up online videos of some of these techniques, such as trimming an artichoke or making a *velouté* sauce.

Italian Sauce

- 2 tablespoons butter
- 1 tablespoon chopped parsley
- ½ tablespoon minced shallots
- ½ tablespoon minced mushrooms
- ½ (750-ml) bottle white wine
- ½ cup *velouté* sauce (recipe follows)
- ¼ cup chicken stock
- 1 teaspoon salt

1. Melt the butter over medium heat in a medium saucepan. Add the parsley, shallots, and mushrooms, and sauté until softened but not browned, about 5 minutes.

2. Add the wine, stir well, and simmer until the sauce is reduced by a quarter.

3. Add the *velouté* and stock. Bring to a boil, then reduce the heat and simmer until it has thickened a bit. Add the salt and adjust seasoning to taste.

4. As soon as the sauce is thick enough to coat the back of a spoon, remove it from the heat.

5. If you make the sauce ahead, warm it in a double boiler when needed.

Velouté Sauce

> Once you've mastered this technique, you'll find it works well for making gravies or other thickened sauces. Very handy!

- 1½ cups chicken or vegetable stock
- 2 tablespoons butter
- 1 tablespoon minced shallot
- 1 sprig fresh thyme
- 3 tablespoons flour
- salt and pepper

1. Heat the stock in a small saucepan until just boiling.

2. In a medium saucepan over medium-low heat, melt the butter and sauté the shallots and thyme until they are softened but not browned, about 3 minutes.

3. Add the flour and stir to combine into a dry paste. Cook for a minute or two, until it's starting to smell toasty but hasn't browned.

4. Add ¼ cup of the stock and whisk until completely incorporated. Continue until you've added all of the stock. (By adding the stock little by little, you avoid lumps.)

5. Bring it up to a near boil, then turn down the heat and simmer until it has thickened to the consistency of gravy, 5 to 10 minutes.

6. Remove from the heat and season to taste with salt and pepper. Strain if you'd like a perfectly smooth sauce; otherwise just take out the thyme stem.

Tidbit of History: Arranging a Ball Buffet

This meal is a mere sample of a full ball menu. Suppers like the one Amy and Laurie attend were extravagant productions, with three to five courses ... and remember, each course wasn't one, but many dishes! If you have the urge to re-create the whole buffet, the famed chef Urbain Dubois gives detailed instructions for arranging the table in his book *Cuisine artistique*. Soup is served first, as the only hot item. The rest of the food is placed symmetrically, with entrées on long platters, alternating with side dishes on round plates. Dubois directs chefs to decorate with plentiful garnishes (like all the truffles you can find), flowers, and ornamental sculptures made of fat. Yes, you read that right; Dubois claims they look as elegant as alabaster. (We'll take his word for it.) According to Dubois, you must never discount the power of fantasy in creating haute cuisine—you must keep innovating because the culinary arts are an infinite, inexhaustible science![8]

8 Dubois, Urbain, *Cuisine artistique: études de l'école moderne* (Paris: Librairie E. Dentu, 1872), 22–26.

Charlotte Russe

There are many variations on charlotte russe, but the general idea is a chilled dessert with a creamy filling and a soft crust of ladyfingers. Nowadays, Bavarian cream is usually an egg custard mixed with whipped cream, but in the 19th-century French recipes we consulted, it was simply whipped cream mixed with some sort of flavoring, usually fruit. They used isinglass (fish gelatin!) to help it set. This is a surprisingly easy recipe if you use store-bought ladyfingers, and either way it looks super-fancy, but we're including all the steps to make one from scratch.

Makes 8 servings

For the ladyfingers:
- 3 large eggs
- ⅔ cup white sugar
- ¼ teaspoon salt
- 1 cup flour
- 2 tablespoons cornstarch
- powdered sugar, for dusting

For the Bavarian cream:
- 1 cup fruit purée (strawberry, raspberry, peach, anything you like—the more exotic, the better!)
- ¼ to 1 cup sugar (adjust depending on the sweetness of the fruit—only something very tart like passionfruit would need the full amount)
- 1 to 2 teaspoons lemon juice (optional; use this if your fruit isn't very tart, or has a dull flavor)
- 1 (¼-ounce) envelope plain powdered gelatin
- 3 cups heavy whipping cream

For assembly:
- fresh fruit, for garnishing

PREPARE THE LADYFINGERS:

1. Put about 2 inches of water in a medium saucepan and bring it to a boil.

2. Preheat the oven to 350°F.

3. In a heatproof bowl (the bowl of your stand mixer is perfect if you're using one), combine the eggs, sugar, and salt. Set it in the top of the pan with the boiling water. The bottom of the bowl should not be in the water—if it is, take some water out, or make a ring of aluminum foil to boost it up.

4. Heat while stirring until the mixture is quite warm, but not bubbling, about 5 minutes.

5. Remove from heat and whip on high speed with the whisk attachment for 5 to 10 minutes until it is very light, foamy, and pale yellow. It will nearly quadruple in volume, and should hold soft peaks.

6. Meanwhile, line two sheet pans with parchment paper.

7. Sift the flour and cornstarch over the egg mixture, and gently fold it in with a spatula, only stirring until the flour is just combined.

8. Spoon the batter into a piping bag fitted with a ½-inch tip (or a sandwich bag with a corner cut off) and pipe 3-inch-long strips onto the baking sheets. They should be about 1 inch wide.

9. Sift a generous amount of powdered sugar over the piped batter.

10. Bake one pan at a time for 10 to 12 minutes, until puffed and set. Allow to cool on the baking sheets.

11. If you are making the ladyfingers ahead, store them in an airtight container so they don't soften.

PREPARE THE BAVARIAN CREAM:

1. While the ladyfingers are cooling: In a small saucepan, combine the fruit purée and sugar to taste, and lemon juice if using. Add the gelatin and heat until the gelatin is dissolved. Allow to cool.

2. Whip the cream to stiff peaks, then gently fold in the fruit purée.

ASSEMBLE THE CHARLOTTE RUSSE:

1. Lightly oil an 8- or 9-inch springform pan, then line the edges with the most attractive of the ladyfingers, bottom sides pointing in. Use the less attractive ones to line the bottom—you may have to break them up a bit to get good coverage.

2. Spoon half of the Bavarian cream into the pan, and smooth it out nicely.

3. Add another layer of ladyfingers, if you have some left. You can also add a layer of chopped fruit if it's not too juicy.

4. Add the rest of the Bavarian cream, and smooth it out.

5. Cover with plastic wrap and refrigerate until set, at least 2 hours or overnight.

6. Remove the charlotte russe from the pan and decorate the top with fresh fruit. *Voilà!*

Tidbit of History: Repast from the Past

A lot of us today expect breakfast in the morning, lunch around noon, and dinner or supper in the evening. While reading *Little Women*, you might have noticed that 19th-century mealtimes, while having familiar names, could mean different expectations from ours. So here's a brief overview of the vocabulary:

Breakfast has been the most consistent in meaning over time; it's traditionally the first meal of the day. The Victorian spread tended to be much heartier than the grab-and-go breakfasts we have now. Take a look on page 144 for the fried fish-balls that Hannah makes in the morning.

Lunch in the Civil War era wasn't the significant midday repast we have today. "Lunch" could mean a quick snack that was easily portable for work or travel (e.g., Hannah's turn-overs, page 136), or it could indicate a party held for friends, especially among women (like Amy's fête for her art classmates, page 86).

Dinner was the most elaborate and important meal of the day. The time depended on the family's schedule and when they could all gather together—it could be anywhere from midday to early evening. Jo's New York boarding house holds their dinner at 5 o'clock (page 54).

Supper, compared to dinner, was relatively light and less structured, but it also usually offered a selection of hot items, in contrast to lunch and tea. Suppers had a social aspect to them and were often tied to formal evening occasions. (Go to page 98 for Amy's Christmas ball supper in France.)

Tea was the final meal of the day, usually with family and occasional friends. Tea had a simpler menu that you could easily add to, in case of unexpected company. (See Happy Surprise Tea on page 160.)

CHAPTER 5

Laurie

"Curly black hair; brown skin; big, black eyes; handsome nose; fine teeth; small hands and feet; taller than I am; very polite, for a boy, and altogether jolly."

CHAPTER 3: "THE LAURENCE BOY"

Is there anyone more charming than Laurie? The answer is no. Theodore Laurence is the definition of the ideal boy next door. When we first meet Laurie, he is rich in money but starving for affection. While the wealthier crowd look down their noses at the Marches in their genteel poverty, Laurie can't believe his good luck that they've adopted him as one of their own, and he goes out of his way to show his gratitude. Laurie is like a lonely, curly-headed puppy who'd been stuck in a gilded cage and has now finally found his humans—he frolics all over with his tail wagging, and he sticks by the family with unwavering devotion. In return for the Marches' kindness, he tactfully offers luxuries that are usually out of their reach, giving the sisters much-needed breaks from work and worry. Mischievous and full of pranks, he makes an excellent BFF for Jo, and their camaraderie (even with the complication of unrequited feelings) is beautiful to behold.

The dishes that readers associate with Laurie reflect who he is: generous, jolly, and somehow both unpretentious and classy at the same time. In the story, Laurie's meals and snacks give him chances to have fun and further cement the bond he has with the Marches. Before they start hanging out, Laurie sends a fine Christmas supper to the girls after they give away their breakfast. (Well, technically, it was his grandfather, but it was Laurie's idea.) Jo cultivates her budding friendship with Laurie when she visits him with a blanc-mange for his sore throat. In the summer, Laurie installs a post office in the hedge between their houses, through which they exchange gifts, including pickles. And when their squad is in full force, Laurie arranges a glorious summer picnic for them all.

Blanc–Mange for Sore Throats

Presently there came a loud ring, then a decided voice, asking for "Mr. Laurie," and a surprised-looking servant came running up to announce a young lady.

"All right, show her up, it's Miss Jo," said Laurie, going to the door of his little parlor to meet Jo, who appeared, looking rosy and kind and quite at her ease, with a covered dish in one hand and Beth's three kittens in the other.

"Here I am, bag and baggage," she said briskly. "Mother sent her love, and was glad if I could do anything for you. Meg wanted me to bring some of her blanc-mange; she makes it very nicely, and Beth thought her cats would be comforting. I knew you'd laugh at them, but I couldn't refuse, she was so anxious to do something."

It so happened that Beth's funny loan was just the thing; for, in laughing over the kits, Laurie forgot his bashfulness, and grew sociable at once.

"That looks too pretty to eat," he said, smiling with pleasure, as Jo uncovered the dish, and showed the blanc-mange, surrounded by a garland of green leaves, and the scarlet flowers of Amy's pet geranium.

"It isn't anything, only they all felt kindly, and wanted to show it. Tell the girl to put it away for your tea: it's so simple you can eat it; and, being soft, it will slip down without hurting your sore throat."

CHAPTER 5: "BEING NEIGHBORLY"

Makes 2 to 4 servings

- 1 tablespoon powdered gelatin or 4 gelatin sheets
- 2 cups whole milk, divided
- 1 egg, beaten
- 3½ tablespoons sugar
- pinch of salt
- zest of 1 lemon

1. In a small bowl, put the gelatin in ½ cup of the milk for 15 minutes to let it bloom.

2. Add a few inches of water to the bottom of a double boiler—make sure the water doesn't touch the top pot—and bring to a boil. Lower the heat to medium-low, so the water is just at a simmer.

3. In a medium bowl, mix the egg and sugar. Whisk in the remaining 1½ cups milk.

4. Put the egg mixture in the top of the double boiler and heat over the simmering water for 20 to 25 minutes, stirring frequently. Taste it to check that it no longer tastes of raw egg—if it does, it needs more time. Take off the heat.

5. Add the salt, gelatin mixture, and lemon zest, and stir until dissolved.

6. Rinse a mold or bowl that will hold at least 2 cups with water, and then strain the blanc-mange mixture into it through a fine-meshed sieve.

7. Let it set in the fridge for a few hours.

8. When you're ready to unmold the blanc-mange, dip it into a bath of hot water for a few seconds till the edges just begin to melt. Invert onto a plate.

Peach Pickles for the P.O.

The P.O. was a capital little institution, and flourished wonderfully, for nearly as many queer things passed through it as through the real [post] office. Tragedies and cravats, poetry and pickles, garden-seeds and long letters, music and gingerbread, rubbers, invitations, scoldings, and puppies. The old gentleman liked the fun, and amused himself by sending odd bundles, mysterious messages, and funny telegrams; and his gardener, who was smitten with Hannah's charms, actually sent a love-letter to Jo's care. How they laughed when the secret came out, never dreaming how many love-letters that little post-office would hold in the years to come.

CHAPTER 10: "THE P.C. AND P.O."

When we think of pickles, we think of cucumbers, but they were just one of the many types of pickles that were eaten in the *Little Women* era—to be honest, they pretty much pickled anything that stood still long enough. These peach pickles are addictively sweet and sour, and easy to make! Look for firm peaches, a little on the unripe side.

Makes about 4 cups

- 3 large peaches
- 4 whole cloves
- 2 cups white or cider vinegar
- ½ cup firmly packed brown sugar

1. Wash the peaches well and rub off any excessive fuzz.

2. Chop them into bite-sized pieces, and put them in jars with the cloves.

3. Combine the vinegar and sugar in a small saucepan and bring to a boil.

4. Pour the vinegar mixture over the peaches and seal the jars.

5. Refrigerate for 3 days, then drain off half the vinegar (don't throw it out—a splash of the vinegar mixed with club soda makes a refreshing drink!) and replace it with water. Refrigerate for another week and your pickles will be ready.

Laurie vs. Professor Bhaer

"Jo" should have remained a literary spinster but so many enthusiastic young ladies wrote to me clamorously demanding that she should marry Laurie, or somebody, that I didn't dare to refuse and out of perversity went and made a funny match for her. I expect vials of wrath to be poured out upon my head, but rather enjoy the prospect. —Louisa May Alcott

The moment Jo hides behind a curtain at a ball and bumps into Laurie is the perfect meet-cute. Their friendship that follows is one for the ages. But when Jo doesn't love Laurie back, it's flabbergasting for us readers. It breaks our hearts because we love Laurie, and we can't imagine how anyone can help feeling otherwise. But this outcome taught us two crucial life lessons:

1. No matter how much you want it, the choice for two people to be together is theirs and no one else's, and

2. You can't make yourself love anyone, no matter how much everyone else wants and expects it, even if you wish you could!

Upon further re-reads, we grudgingly get it. Jo and Laurie wouldn't have enough in common to live happily as a couple for one fundamental reason: Jo needs to struggle. She lives for the fight. Laurie, on the other hand, would want to pave the way for her.

In contrast, Professor Bhaer challenges Jo and sees her true self in a way that Laurie never would. The professor's cozy, untidy, absent-minded ways suit Jo perfectly, and though he isn't swoonily handsome like Laurie, he is "attractive as a genial fire, and people seemed to gather about him as naturally as about a warm hearth." Yes, he is rather snobbish about her sensationalist stories, but in this he's really just a mouthpiece for Alcott's personal ambivalence about her own writing career.

If Jo had married Laurie, she would've had a tough time finding a purpose as a well-to-do housewife. In the sequels, *Little Men* and *Jo's Boys*, you see how Jo achieves her ideal of a fulfilling, important career as an educator and writer with a complementary, patient partner striving for the same goals alongside her.

Advantage: Team Bhaer.

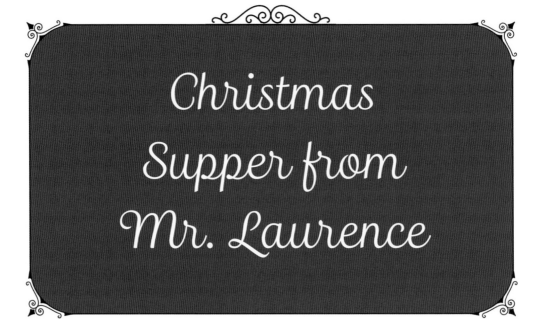

Christmas Supper from Mr. Laurence

The excitement had hardly subsided, when Hannah appeared, with "Mrs. March's compliments, and would the ladies walk down to supper."

This was a surprise, even to the actors; and when they saw the table, they looked at one another in rapturous amazement. It was like Marmee to get up a little treat for them; but anything so fine as this was unheard-of since the departed days of plenty. There was ice-cream,—actually two dishes of it, pink and white,—and cake and fruit and distracting French bonbons, and, in the middle of the table, four great bouquets of hot-house flowers!

It quite took their breath away; and they stared first at the table and then at their mother, who looked as if she enjoyed it immensely.

"Is it fairies?" asked Amy.

"It's Santa Claus," said Beth.

"Mother did it", and Meg smiled her sweetest, in spite of her gray beard and white eyebrows.

"Aunt March had a good fit and sent the supper," cried Jo, with a sudden inspiration.

"All wrong. Old Mr. Laurence sent it," replied Mrs. March.

"The Laurence boy's grandfather! What in the world put such a thing into his head? We don't know him!" exclaimed Meg.

CHAPTER 2: "A MERRY CHRISTMAS"

Having given up their Christmas breakfast to a poor family, the girls are unexpectedly rewarded with a dainty array of treats after they perform the play they've been rehearsing. It turns out their scary old, rich neighbor, Mr. Laurence (or possibly his handsome young grandson?) heard about their good deed and sent over a marvelous feast. In their reduced financial circumstances, this is utmost luxury. Two kinds of ice cream? Flowers in the middle of winter? So fancy!

Pink Ice Cream (Currant and Lemon)

The original recipe suggests you color it with cochineal, a food dye that's made from insects. While cochineal is still used today in many foods, the currant jelly does a perfectly fine job of making the ice cream pink. If you want a brighter color, by all means feel free to use any food coloring you like.

Makes 4 to 6 servings

- ½ cup red currant jelly (to make your own, see page 33)
- ¼ cup corn syrup
- juice of 1 small lemon
- 2 cups cream
- few drops of red food coloring (optional)

1. Whisk together the jelly and corn syrup, then whisk in the lemon juice, then the cream. Whisk in the food coloring, if using.

2. Freeze in an ice cream maker (hand-crank for authenticity, or electric for convenience), then allow to harden in the freezer for at least an hour before serving.

White Ice Cream (Almond and Rose)

The combination of almond and rose is intriguing and difficult to identify if you're tasting it for the first time. It has a distinctly old-fashioned flavor, lovely but clearly from another era.

Makes 4 to 6 servings

- 1 tablespoon arrowroot powder
- 1 cup milk
- 1 cup cream
- ½ cup sugar
- ¼ teaspoon almond extract
- 2 teaspoons rose water

1. Mix the arrowroot in a small dish with enough milk to make a thin paste. Make sure there are no lumps.

2. Heat the remaining milk and cream in a medium saucepan over medium heat until it boils.

3. Stir in the arrowroot and bring it back to a boil.

4. Stir in the sugar, briefly boil again, and remove from the heat.

5. Refrigerate the mixture overnight, or until it's entirely cold.

6. Add the almond extract and rose water, and freeze using an ice-cream maker (hand-crank for authenticity, or electric for convenience).

7. Transfer into a storage container and freeze until firm.

Friendly Advice: Look for Ahmed brand rose water, which has a gentle rose scent and isn't strongly perfumed. If you use another brand such as Cortas or Sadaf, start with ¼ teaspoon and add more if you like. The almond and rose flavors should balance each other, as if combining to make a third flavor.

Fine Cake

This is based on a recipe called Federal Cake, which some say goes back to Alexander Hamilton's Federalist political party. They were often cut into small diamond-shaped cakes, but this one is more like a pound cake loaf— old-fashioned and rich, just like Mr. Laurence. Use any kind of raisins you like, or other chopped dried fruit. Dried apricots are especially good here.

Makes 8 servings

- ¼ cup brandy, apple cider, or some other liquid if you prefer
- 8 ounces (1½ cups) raisins
- 8 ounces butter
- 8 ounces (1 cup) sugar
- ½ teaspoon freshly grated nutmeg
- 2 eggs
- ½ teaspoon baking soda
- ½ cup sour cream
- 8 ounces (2¼ cups) flour

1. Have all the ingredients at room temperature.

2. Preheat oven to 375°F and grease a 9 x 5-inch loaf pan with butter or nonstick spray.

3. Combine the brandy or other liquid and raisins in a small bowl and set aside.

4. Cream the butter, sugar, and nutmeg together with a hand mixer or stand mixer.

5. Add the eggs and beat on medium to high speed for 3 to 5 minutes, until it is fluffy and light-colored.

6. Stir the baking soda into the sour cream and beat in.

7. Drain the brandy from the raisins and add the brandy to the mixture.

8. Add the flour in four parts, mixing just until incorporated. Make sure to scrape down the sides of the bowl as you mix.

9. When you get to the last part of the flour, toss the raisins in the flour and add them along with it.

10. Spoon batter into the prepared pan and bake until a toothpick inserted in the middle of the cake comes out clean. Baking time can vary widely depending on the pan and your oven—start testing at 45 minutes but it can take as long as 90 minutes. If you notice the top browning before it's set in the middle, cover with foil and keep baking.

Distracting French Bonbons

French bonbons were little candies wrapped in colorful paper, printed with "mottoes," such as little sayings, poems, or predictions, much like fortune cookies.

Makes 20 to 30 pieces, but some might not look nice enough to use

- butter, for greasing
- 1 cup sugar
- 1 tablespoon brandy, plus more for soaking

1. Thoroughly butter a cookie sheet. Also butter a butter knife and keep it ready.

2. Melt the sugar in a small saucepan over low heat. As it melts, tilt the pan back and forth to move the sugar around, rather than stirring with a spoon. Watch carefully to make sure it doesn't burn, but you do want a nice caramel color. Once the sugar has melted, clip a candy thermometer to the side of the pan.

3. Keep the sugar on the heat until it gets to the hard crack stage (300°F). Remove from the heat, then stand back and stir quickly as you add the brandy because it can spatter.

4. Pour the melted sugar onto the buttered cookie sheet and tilt this way and that until it makes a sheet about ⅛- to ¼-inch thick.

5. Stand by for the candy to reach the exact time it's ready to score into bite-sized squares—there is a moment you can easily miss, where it's soft enough to mark but hard enough for the knife lines to stay. Start with the outer edges and move inward as it cools, making a grid of indented lines.

6. When the candy has cooled, you can remove it from the cookie sheet with a thin spatula and snap the pieces apart. Try lightly tapping along the lines with the back of your buttered knife. Some will probably break in the wrong place, which is fine.

7. Once they are snapped apart, wipe them with a paper towel or cloth soaked in brandy—this intensifies the brandy flavor and helps keep them from sticking to each other or the paper.

8. Wrap in thin tissue paper, then wrap in colorful paper with a motto inside.

Jolly Picnic Lunch at Camp Laurence

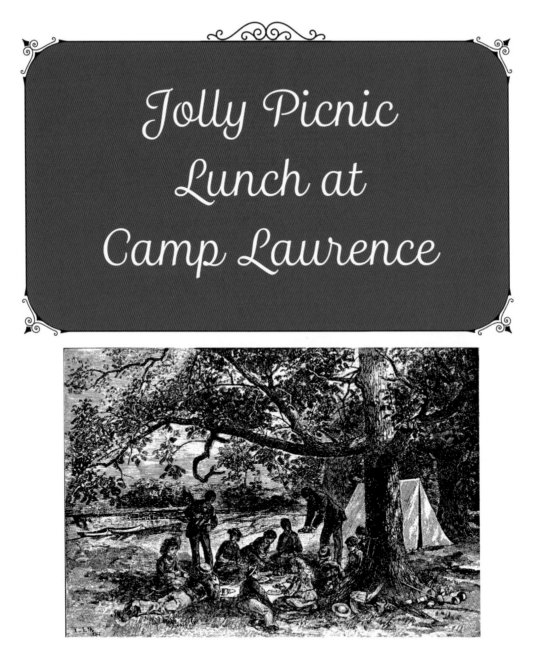

Dear Jo, What ho!

Some English girls and boys are coming to see me to-morrow and I want to have a jolly time. If it's fine, I'm going to pitch my tent in Longmeadow, and row up the whole crew to lunch and croquet,—have a fire, make messes, gypsy fashion, and all sorts of larks. They are nice people, and like such things. Brooke will go, to keep us boys steady, and Kate Vaughn will play propriety for the girls. I want you all to come; can't let Beth off at any price, and nobody shall worry her. Don't bother about rations,—I'll see to that and everything else,—only do come, there's a good fellow!

In a tearing hurry,

Yours ever, LAURIE.

CHAPTER 12: "CAMP LAURENCE"

Laurie has guests visiting from England, so he decides to invite everyone for a big outdoor picnic! Unladylike Jo and Laurie's boorish friend Fred Vaughn do not make a good impression on each other, and things are a little tense until Laurie breaks out the picnic lunch. It's always a little awkward introducing your different friend groups to each other—you never know who's going to show up in a ridiculous hat or who's going to cheat at croquet … but if you bring lots of good food, everything will probably work out okay in the end.

Since the book doesn't specify what they ate at the picnic (other than coffee, page 140, and berries and cream, which Laurie of course takes as an opportunity to tease Jo about her disastrous dinner party, page 46), we chose a variety of fare that sounded delicious and portable. This meal is one of our favorites, with big pillowy potato rolls, potted ham (we'd never tried it before, but it is amazing), a crisp cucumber salad, gorgeous magenta pickled eggs, and a nice lemon pound cake. Note to self: Put Laurie in charge of all the picnics.

Hearty Potato Rolls

Why add mashed potatoes to bread? They give it a softer, fluffier texture, a slightly sweet flavor, and help keep it from going stale as quickly. These rolls make excellent sandwiches and would be perfect for hamburger buns (although hamburgers weren't invented until the 1880s).

Makes 16 large rolls

- 2 medium russet potatoes (about 2 cups mashed)
- 1 tablespoon butter
- 1 tablespoon salt
- 2 egg yolks
- 1½ cups milk, warmed, plus more for glazing
- 1 packet active dry yeast (2¼ teaspoons)
- about 6½ cups flour

1. Boil the potatoes, skins on, until they are soft all the way through and the skins are beginning to split.

2. Drain the water and return the potatoes to the pot. Let them sit with the lid on for 15 minutes to an hour (whenever you get back to them), which lets them absorb any extra water and become fluffier.

3. Remove the skins and mash the potatoes in a large bowl with the butter and salt.

Make sure they are very smooth, with no lumps.

4. Mix in the egg yolks.

5. Mix in the warm milk and yeast. Let it sit until you see the yeast starting to bubble.

6. Gradually knead in the flour, until the dough is smooth. The amount of flour you need may vary a bit depending on how moist your potatoes are. The dough will be fairly soft, but you should be able to stretch an edge of the dough until it's translucent without tearing (this is called the "windowpane test").

7. Oil the bowl and put the dough back in. Allow to rise until doubled in volume, about 1 hour in a warm place (75°F is ideal) or overnight in the refrigerator.

8. Punch down the dough and divide it into 16 pieces.

9. Form each piece into a tight ball (smooth on top and tucked in tightly underneath) and place them on two parchment-covered sheet pans, about 1 inch apart.

10. Cover with oiled plastic wrap and let rise in a warm place for about an hour, or until doubled in size. They should now be touching each other a bit.

11. Preheat the oven to 350°F.

12. Brush the tops of the rolls with milk.

13. Bake for 20 to 25 minutes, until golden brown and about 200°F to 205°F internally.

Potted Ham

Potted ham isn't common in the U.S. anymore, and it's too bad because it's wonderful. It makes a great sandwich spread, or you could serve it as an hors d'oeuvre with crackers. A Victorian cookbook advises, "A jar of this will be found useful to travellers in remote places"—perfect for an outing to Camp Laurence! If you want to be extra-authentic, you'd seal the top of each container with melted lard instead of butter, but really the butter is much tastier.

Makes 4 to 6 servings

- 8 ounces cooked uncured dinner ham, with any gristle, sinew, or chunks of fat discarded
- 7 tablespoons plus 6 tablespoons unsalted butter, divided
- ¼ teaspoon cayenne pepper
- ⅛ teaspoon ground mace
- ⅛ teaspoon nutmeg

1. Chop the ham into 1-inch cubes or smaller.

2. In a small saucepan, melt 7 tablespoons of the butter.

3. Put the ham in a food processor, along with the cayenne pepper, mace, nutmeg, and the melted butter. Blend until mostly smooth, but not totally pasty. The ham should have a finely minced texture. Pack the ham into 3 (½-cup) ramekins.

4. In a small saucepan, melt the remaining 6 tablespoons butter and top each ramekin with 2 tablespoons of it.

5. Cover and refrigerate just until the butter is solid, and then serve.

6. To freeze, cover in plastic wrap, and the potted ham will keep up to 3 months. Defrost overnight in the fridge, then let it come up to room temperature before serving.

Friendly Advice: Try making a second batch with cooked chicken breast instead of ham (you'll need to add salt), then pack the two in alternating layers. Fancy!

Wholesome Cucumbers

A refreshing, simple salad, perfect as a light summer side.

Makes 3 servings

- 1 English cucumber
- 1 tablespoon apple cider vinegar
- salt and pepper

1. Peel and slice the cucumber very thin. Put the slices in fresh cold water to crisp them.

2. Once you are ready to eat, drain the cucumbers, put them in a dish, and mix with the vinegar.

3. Sprinkle with salt and pepper to taste, and serve.

Get the Receipt

Victorians' produce choices might have been limited during certain seasons, but when they did have vegetables, they could be much fresher than what we're used to. Check out the original recipe for these cucumbers from Mrs. Cornelius:

> Cucumbers should be gathered while dew is yet on them, and put immediately into water. Half an hour before dinner, pare and slice them very thin, and let them lie in fresh water till dinner is ready; then drain them, lay them into a dish, sprinkle them with salt, pour on the vinegar, and add the pepper last.

Laurie

Pickled Eggs

> This is Mrs. Cornelius's original method, but most modern recipes for pickled eggs include 3 tablespoons of sugar, and some also add sliced onion. We like the original way, but if you're already used to eating pickled eggs, you might miss the sugar.

Makes 4 eggs

- 4 eggs
- 1 medium beet
- 1 cup apple cider vinegar
- 5 whole cloves
- 1 teaspoon black peppercorns
- 1 teaspoon salt
- ¼ teaspoon freshly grated nutmeg

1. Put the eggs in a small saucepan with enough water to cover them. Put the lid on and bring to a boil, then turn off the heat and let them sit for 15 minutes. (If you have a pressure cooker, cooking the eggs in it works very well and makes them easy to peel.)

2. Trim the top and bottom of the beet, and cut it in quarters. Put it in a small saucepan with about an inch of water, cover, and boil on high heat until the beet is soft, about 15 minutes.

3., Allow the beet to cool a bit, then trim off the peel and chop it into ½-inch cubes. Place the cubes in a medium bowl with the vinegar, cloves, peppercorns, salt, and nutmeg.

4. Shell the eggs, and put them into a 1-pint jar. Add the beets and vinegar mixture.

5. Refrigerate for three days before serving.

Pound Cake

It's called a pound cake because originally you used a pound each of butter, sugar, flour, and eggs. This one is scaled down by half.

Makes about 12 servings

- 8 ounces butter
- 8 ounces (1 cup) sugar
- 4 eggs
- zest of 1 lemon
- 8 ounces (2¼ cups) flour
- pinch of salt
- juice of 1 lemon, divided
- about ½ cup powdered sugar, sifted
- ¼ teaspoon almond extract (optional)

1. Have all the ingredients at room temperature—this is important to keep the batter from curdling.

2. Preheat the oven to 350°F and grease a 9 x 5-inch loaf pan with butter or cooking spray.

3. Cream the butter and sugar together with a hand mixer or stand mixer until light and fluffy, about 5 minutes.

4. Add the eggs one at a time, and whip at high speed for 3 minutes after adding each one, until the mixture is smooth and light, like whipped cream. If it looks curdled, keep whipping.

5. When you add the last egg, add the lemon zest as well, and beat for 10 minutes, stopping occasionally to scrape down the sides.

6. Add one-third of the flour along with the salt and half of the lemon juice, and beat on high for just a few seconds, until combined. Add one-third more flour, beat on high until just combined, then do the same with the final third.

7. Pour the batter into the prepared pan and bake for about 1 hour, or until the top is golden brown and a skewer inserted into the middle comes out clean. (Baking times can vary a lot, so start checking at 45 minutes, but it might take up to 75.)

8. For the glaze, mix the remaining lemon juice with the powdered sugar in a small bowl until it's the consistency you like. Make sure to sift the sugar well first, then add a little juice slowly to make a smooth paste before you add the rest. Add almond extract. Drizzle over the cake and allow to set before serving.

Laurie

CHAPTER 6

The March Family

"We can't give up our girls for a dozen fortunes. Rich or poor,
we will keep together and be happy in one another."

CHAPTER 4: "BURDENS"

When we read Little Women, we're all Laurie, peering through a window into the Marches' snug homelife and wishing for a spot by their fireplace. Their household is one of the coziest in all fiction, and the Marches show us how much power there is to a close-knit family. They aren't perfect; each individual member has faults and flaws, and they have their share of spats and sadness. But they all complement and learn from each other, and together they create an enviable place of warmth and support. Also, the Marches stick to their strong beliefs, even if their views aren't fashionable. All their moralizing can admittedly become a bit much sometimes, but they sure don't lack conviction! And watching them encourages us readers to fearlessly champion our ideas and principles, whether they're trendy or not.

March family meals are about togetherness and charity. Hannah's home cooking takes center stage on the dinner table, full of love and consideration for the people she devotedly serves. The girls are reminded of their good fortune when they give their breakfast to neighbors on Christmas Day. The Marches also have special reunions: a joyous Christmas dinner when Mr. March comes home, a tea celebrating Amy and Laurie's surprise homecoming, and an apple-picking holiday for Marmee's 60th birthday. Their feasts are displays of gratitude, especially after long stretches of being apart, and they easily draw lonely outsiders into their comfortable circle.

Hannah's Plain Wholesome Vittles

DEAR MIS MARCH,—

I jes drop a line to say we git on fust rate. The girls is clever and fly round right smart. Miss Meg is going to make a proper good housekeeper; she hes the liking for it, and gits the hang of things surprisin quick. Jo doos beat all for goin ahead, but she don't stop to cal'k'late fust, and you never know where she's like to bring up. She done out a tub of clothes on Monday, but she starched 'em afore they was wrenched, and blued a pink calico dress till I thought I should a died a laughin. Beth is the best of little creeters, and a sight of help to me, bein so forehanded and dependable. She tries to learn everything, and really goes to market beyond her years; likewise keeps accounts, with my help, quite wonderful. We have got on very economical so fur; I don't let the girls hev coffee only once a week, accordin to your wish, and keep em on plain wholesome vittles. Amy does well about frettin, wearin her best clothes and eatin sweet stuff. Mr. Laurie is as full of didoes as usual, and turns the house upside down frequent; but he heartens up the girls, and so I let em hev full swing. The old gentleman sends heaps of things, and is rather wearin, but means wal, and it aint my place to say nothin. My bread is riz, so no more at this time. I send my duty to Mr. March, and hope he's seen the last of his Pewmonia.

"Yours Respectful,

"HANNAH MULLET."

CHAPTER 16: "LETTERS"

Hannah has been with the family since Meg was a baby, and she is "more a friend than a servant." She's worked for the Marches since before they lost their money but, faithful creature that she is, decides to stick with them. Hannah takes care of most of the housework and cooking, which is backbreaking labor in these times. She stays in the background of the story, but if we're talking about the Marches' meals, she is the star of the production. Hannah cares deeply for the sisters, and she bakes their daily bread with great affection. Fiercely protective, she looks after the girls in their parents' absence, making sure to keep them on "plain wholesome vittles."

Hot Turn-Overs, or "Muffs"

There was a momentary lull, broken by Hannah, who stalked in, laid two hot turn-overs on the table, and stalked out again. These turn-overs were an institution; and the girls called them "muffs," for they had no others, and found the hot pies very comforting to their hands on cold mornings.

Hannah never forgot to make them, no matter how busy or grumpy she might be, for the walk was long and bleak; the poor things got no other lunch and were seldom home before two.

CHAPTER 4: "BURDENS"

In Victorian times, ladies would carry around a muff, a cylinder of fur to warm their hands on cold winter days. Since the sisters don't have any, Hannah makes them hot turn-overs—both as a convenient, portable snack and to keep their hands warm. Aw, Hannah can be a grouch sometimes, but she's a soft-hearted sweetie who's always looking out for you. She probably uses a simple crust that's not too flaky or buttery, and rolls it out thick to keep the "muffs" from crumbling in pockets. Turn-overs were often fried back then, but Hannah would bake hers, since she wouldn't want to stain the girls' clothes!

Makes 8 turn-overs

- 3 tart apples, like Granny Smith
- 4 or 5 tablespoons water
- 2 or 3 tablespoons packed brown sugar
- scant ½ teaspoon nutmeg
- 1 tablespoon butter
- 1 Double Pie Crust (page 63)
- extra flour for rolling

1. Core and peel the apples, and slice them small and thin.

2. Heat a very large skillet over high heat until hot, then lower to medium-high. Put in the water, and then the apples. Cook for about 4 minutes, or until some of the apples are limp, but others are still a bit stiff.

3. Add the brown sugar and nutmeg. Cook for 2 more minutes, mixing occasionally with a wooden spoon.

4. Add the butter, mix, and cook 1 more minute. Take off the heat and set aside.

5. Preheat the oven to 400°F.

6. Flour a large, clean surface and your rolling pin. Roll out the pie dough, repairing any cracks by pressing them together, until it's ¼ inch thick.

Cut into 4 x 4-inch squares. Scoop about 2 tablespoons stewed apple into the center of each square, and then fold them from corner to corner into a triangle, pressing and crimping the edges together with a fork. (If you find the dough hard to manage, folding in half into rectangles is easier, although the result might not be as cute.)

7. Place the turn-overs on a baking sheet 1 inch apart. Poke a few holes into each turn-over with a fork or knife. Optional: Hannah probably wouldn't have done this, but the turn-overs are even nicer if you brush the tops with milk and sprinkle them with sugar before baking.

8. Bake for 15 minutes in the preheated oven until the edges are browned. Lower the temperature to 350°F and bake for another 5 minutes.

Friendly Advice: Your sliced apples should have enough room that you can mix them easily in the skillet. If you don't have a very large skillet and your apples are overcrowded, split the batch into two skillets over two burners. If you have any leftover pie crust, make pie crust cookies! Roll out the dough, cut into shapes of your choice, sprinkle with sugar and preferred spices, and bake for 8 to 10 minutes at 350°F.

The March Family

Cale-Cannon

[Mr. Davis] did not soon forget the reproachful glance Amy gave him, as she went, without a word to any one, straight into the ante-room, snatched her things, and left the place "forever," as she passionately declared to herself. She was in a sad state when she got home; and when the older girls arrived, some time later, an indignation meeting was held at once. Mrs. March did not say much, but looked disturbed, and comforted her afflicted little daughter in her tenderest manner. Meg bathed the insulted hand with glycerine and tears; Beth felt that even her beloved kittens would fail as a balm for griefs like this; Jo wrathfully proposed that Mr. Davis be arrested without delay; and Hannah shook her fist at the "villain," and pounded potatoes for dinner as if she had him under her pestle.

CHAPTER 7: "AMY'S VALLEY OF HUMILIATION"

In the late 1840s, there were huge numbers of Irish women fleeing from the Great Famine to the U.S. There are theories that Hannah is Irish, although the evidence is inconclusive. Irish servants had a huge influence on Victorian American cookery. In middle-class kitchens, they avoided plain potatoes and preferred to serve dishes like this cale-cannon (more commonly known as colcannon).[9]

Makes 6 servings

- ½ head of cabbage, about 1½ pounds
- ¼ cup salt, divided, plus more for seasoning
- 3 pounds russet potatoes, peeled and halved
- ½ cup (1 stick) butter, melted
- 1 teaspoon pepper, or to taste

---

9   Veit, *Food in the Civil War Era*, 12–14.

1. Core and cut the cabbage into four pieces. Separate the leaves.

2. In a large pot, starting in cold water with about 2 tablespoons of salt, boil the cabbage leaves for 10 to 15 minutes.

3. In a second large pot, starting in cold water with about 2 tablespoons of salt, boil the potatoes for 20 to 25 minutes.

4. Drain the cabbage and squeeze out excess water, then mince it very small.

5. Drain and mash the potatoes, then gradually mix in cabbage, butter, pepper, and 1 teaspoon salt, or to taste.

Friendly Advice: If the potatoes seem too dry, add a little warm milk.

Coffee as a Treat

"It seems as if half the house was gone," added Meg forlornly.

Beth opened her lips to say something, but could only point to the pile of nicely-mended hose which lay on mother's table, showing that even in her last hurried moments she had thought and worked for them. It was a little thing, but it went straight to their hearts, and in spite of their brave resolutions, they all broke down and cried bitterly.

Hannah wisely allowed them to relieve their feelings, and, when the shower showed signs of clearing up, she came to the rescue, armed with a coffee-pot.

"Now, my dear young ladies, remember what your ma said, and don't fret. Come and have a cup of coffee all round, and then let's fall to work, and be a credit to the family."

Coffee was a treat, and Hannah showed great tact in making it that morning. No one could resist her persuasive nods, or the fragrant invitation issuing from the nose of the coffee-pot. They drew up to the table, exchanged their handkerchiefs for napkins, and in ten minutes were all right again.

CHAPTER 16: "LETTERS"

Here's another example of what a wonderful human Hannah is. She knows the girls and is considerate enough to figure out when they might need a break or a little push. Giving them coffee does both—it cheers the sisters up while giving them a boost of energy.

Before coffee filters, there were various methods of keeping the grounds out of the cup, including boiling it with raw egg or fish skin! It seems bizarre to mix an egg into your coffee, but it does make it especially smooth and removes some of the bitterness, as well as collecting all the grounds. Don't worry, there's no egg flavor left behind.

Makes 4 cups

- 4 cups water
- ½ cup ground coffee
- 1 egg, shell included

1. Put the water in a medium saucepan and over medium heat until warm but not yet boiling.

2. While the water is heating, put the coffee in a small bowl and crack the egg in. Break up the eggshell with your fingers and add it to the bowl, mixing everything together.

3. Add the coffee mixture to the pot and bring it to a boil.

4. Boil for 3 minutes, being careful not to let it boil over. Don't stir it; let the coffee and egg clump together.

5. Turn off the heat and allow to sit for 5 minutes.

6. Strain into cups and serve.

The March Family

Good Family Bread

My bread is riz, so no more at this time. I send my duty to Mr. March, and hope he's seen the last of his Pewmonia.

CHAPTER 16: "LETTERS"

A basic bread recipe would have been the cornerstone of any cook's repertoire, and the original text from Mrs. Cornelius is full of digressions about the moral superiority of baking your own bread. It makes a hearty white loaf, perfect for sandwiches, bread-pudding, or that weird asparagus toast dish on page 53 (trust us, it's really good!). You can easily double this recipe if you like.

Makes 1 loaf

For the sponge:

- 3 tablespoons cornmeal
- 1 teaspoon salt
- 1½ cups water
- ½ cup milk
- ½ teaspoon active dry yeast
- 1 cup flour (5 ounces)

For the bread:

- 3 cups flour (15 ounces), plus a bit more for kneading
- 1 tablespoon kosher salt
- about 2 teaspoons olive oil or vegetable oil for greasing
- milk, for brushing

PREPARE THE SPONGE:

1. The night before you want to bake the bread, boil the cornmeal, salt, and water in a small pot over medium heat until the cornmeal is softened and the mixture thickens, 3 to 5 minutes.

2. Stir in the milk and allow to cool to room temperature.

3. Transfer to a large bowl, and mix in the yeast and flour. Cover and let stand overnight in a warm place (about 75°F is ideal). This is your sponge.

PREPARE THE BREAD:

1. The next day, add the 3 cups flour to the sponge and mix well. Cover and let it rest 30 minutes.

2. Add the kosher salt.

3. Knead the dough by hand or in a stand mixer until it feels silky and not too sticky. You should be able to stretch an edge of the dough until it's translucent without tearing (this is called the "windowpane test"). This should take 10 to 15 minutes. As you knead, add flour as needed, but not so much that the dough becomes stiff.

4. Oil the bowl you were using (no need to wash it) and put the dough in, turning it to coat.

5. Cover and let rise for 1 hour in a warm place.

6. Grease a 9 x 5-inch loaf pan with oil.

7. Once the dough has grown puffy (if you poke it, it should stay poked and not spring back) and has nearly doubled in size, gently punch it down.

8. Remove the dough from the bowl and place it on a floured surface. Spread it out in a more or less rectangular shape, and press out any large bubbles. Roll it tightly lengthwise. Flip the loaf over so the seam is on the bottom, and tuck the long ends underneath so you have a tight loaf shape. Place it in the greased loaf pan, seam-side down.

9. Cover the dough with a damp towel or oiled plastic wrap and let rise for 1 hour, or until puffy and nearly doubled in size.

10. Preheat the oven to 375°F.

11. Brush the top of the loaf with milk. Make a deep slash along the top with a serrated knife, and immediately put it in the oven.

12. Bake 30 to 45 minutes, or until the loaf is browned and the internal temperature rises above 190°F; 200°F to 205°F is usually when the crust will be nicely browned.

13. Remove the loaf from the pan immediately and lay it on its side to cool.

Friendly Advice: If you prefer a tender crust, wrap the loaf in a towel while cooling and the steam will soften it.

Prosey Fish-Balls

"Will Miss Amy ride in her coop (*coupé*), and use all them lovely silver dishes that's stored away over yander?"

"Shouldn't wonder if she drove six white horses, ate off gold plate, and wore diamonds and point-lace every day. Teddy thinks nothing too good for her," returned Jo with infinite satisfaction.

"No more there is! Will you have hash or fish-balls for breakfast?" asked Hannah, who wisely mingled poetry and prose.

CHAPTER 43: "SURPRISES"

Do you like fish sticks? Do you like mashed potatoes? If you answered yes to both of these questions, try these Victorian fish-balls! They taste like creamy, potatoey fish sticks, and you eat them for breakfast. This recipe takes the old-fashioned route of using dry salt cod, which is a specialty item that can be hard to find and a whole process to use. (If you want to take a shortcut, you could poach some fresh white fish, season it with salt, and mince it. We would not judge you for it.) We get the impression that cooks made fish-balls when there were leftover potatoes on hand. Salt cod was a staple in New England, so it was probably a dish that good old Hannah could whip up readily in the morning.

Makes 4 or 5 servings

- 1½ pounds bone-in dry salt cod
- 1½ pounds russet potatoes
- 2 tablespoons salt, plus more for seasoning
- 3 tablespoons milk
- 2 tablespoons melted butter
- pepper
- ⅓ cup flour
- your favorite fat for frying; opt for lard, beef drippings, or rendered salt pork for authenticity

24 HOURS BEFORE COOKING:

1. Soak the salt cod. Cut the cod into large pieces, so they fit easily in a pot. Wash all the salt off the cod under running water, rubbing the fish gently with your fingers. Fill a large container, preferably glass or ceramic, full of water. Set the cod in, cover, and put in the fridge. The cod needs to soak for 24 hours. Change the water every 8 hours, making sure to cover and return it to the fridge.

2. Make the mashed potatoes (this can be done ahead). Peel and quarter the potatoes, and boil them with the 2 tablespoons salt until fork-tender. Drain thoroughly. Victorian recipes recommend leaving them overnight, but you can dry the potatoes quickly by putting them back in the pot and warming them over low heat, shaking frequently and vigorously so the bottom doesn't burn. Mash the potatoes with the milk, melted butter, and a little more salt if needed, but remember the cod will be salty.

WHEN YOU'RE READY TO COOK:

1. When the cod has finished soaking, drain the water. Measure the thickest part of the fish—you will poach it for 10 minutes for every inch of thickness. Fill a large pot with fresh water. Put the cod in the pot, and turn the heat to high. As soon as it boils, lower the heat to a simmer and gently poach the fish.

2. When the cod is cooked, lift it onto a cutting board. Skin and debone the fish while it's still warm—it's easiest to use your fingers, so you can find all the little bones. Using a sharp knife, mince the fish very small.

3. Mix the minced fish thoroughly into the mashed potatoes, and add plenty of pepper. Roll the mixture into balls. Each ball should be about 2 ounces in weight. Flatten a little into discs. Roll lightly in the flour.

4. Fill a deep frying pan with at least 1½ inches of your favorite frying fat and turn to medium-high heat. When the fat barely starts to smoke, add the fish-balls. Fry for 3 to 4 minutes on each side until it's a nice golden brown. Drain on paper towels, and serve immediately.

The March Family

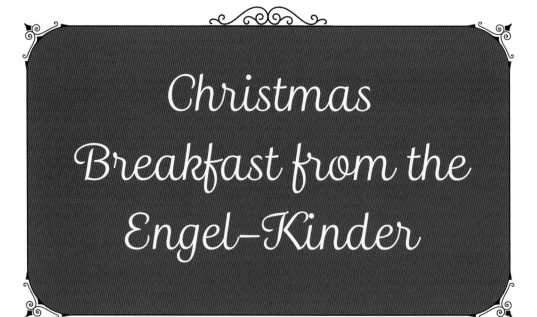

Christmas Breakfast from the Engel-Kinder

"Merry Christmas, little daughters! I'm glad you began at once, and hope you will keep on. But I want to say one word before we sit down. Not far away from here lies a poor woman with a little new-born baby. Six children are huddled into one bed to keep from freezing, for they have no fire. There is nothing to eat over there; and the oldest boy came to tell me they were suffering hunger and cold. My girls, will you give them your breakfast as a Christmas present?"

They were all unusually hungry, having waited nearly an hour, and for a minute no one spoke; only a minute, for Jo exclaimed impetuously,—"I'm so glad you came before we began!"

CHAPTER 2: "A MERRY CHRISTMAS"

A letter from their father on Christmas Eve has just reminded Meg, Jo, Beth, and Amy to be more selfless, and they promise to try with tears in their eyes. Their resolve is tested the very next morning when Marmee suggests that they give away their special Christmas breakfast. After the briefest hesitation (where we imagine they're taking a moment to mourn their rare treats), the sisters pack up the meal with admirable enthusiasm, especially considering they've already been waiting to eat for an hour and are probably getting pretty hangry. The Marches deliver their presents to the Hummels, an impoverished German family living in a freezing room with no food or heat. In their gratitude, the little Hummel children call them *Engel-kinder*, or "angel children," and the sisters are reminded of how lucky they are. This scene pushes us readers to remember that we don't need to have everything to donate something, and that Christmas should be a day to give rather than receive.

Buckwheat Cakes

Meg was already covering the buckwheats, and piling the bread into one big plate.

CHAPTER 2: "A MERRY CHRISTMAS"

> Mrs. Cornelius has a variety of methods for buckwheat cakes, including one that uses only buckwheat flour, buttermilk, and baking soda. That version isn't bad at all, but the addition of an egg makes for a much lighter, fluffier pancake.

Makes about 12 small cakes

- 1 cup buckwheat flour
- ½ teaspoon baking soda
- ¼ teaspoon salt
- 1 tablespoon sugar
- 1 egg
- 1 cup buttermilk
- butter, for the pan, plus more for serving
- maple syrup, for serving

1. Preheat a frying pan over medium-low heat.

2. Whisk the flour, baking soda, salt, and sugar together in a medium bowl.

3. In a small bowl, beat the egg into the buttermilk, then pour over dry ingredients and whisk until mixed. It will be rather thick compared to regular pancake batter.

4. Melt the butter in the hot pan and drop in spoonfuls of batter.

5. Cook until bubbles start to form, 2 or 3 minutes for small (2 to 3-inch diameter) cakes. They will cook rather quickly, so pay attention!

6. Flip over and cook about another minute—you will see the cakes puff up slightly.

7. Serve with butter and maple syrup.

Amy's Muffins

"I shall take the cream and the muffins," added Amy, heroically giving up the articles she most liked.

CHAPTER 2: "A MERRY CHRISTMAS"

> These are what we think of as English muffins, not the sweet cakey kind. They are delicious right out of the pan, but even better toasted. It's not surprising that they would be Amy's favorite!

Makes about 12 muffins

- 2 cups milk
- 1 tablespoon butter
- 1 packet active dry yeast (2¼ teaspoons)
- 1 egg
- 2½ cups flour
- 1½ teaspoons salt
- jam and butter, or clotted cream, for serving

1. In a small saucepan over medium heat, warm the milk and butter together just until the butter begins to melt. Don't let it get too hot—if you dip your finger in, it shouldn't be uncomfortable.

2. Transfer the milk mixture to a large bowl. Stir until the butter is completely melted, then add the yeast.

3. Let sit in a warm place until the yeast dissolves, about 5 minutes.

4. Meanwhile, beat the egg with a fork in a small bowl until foamy.

5. Stir the egg into the milk, then add in the flour and salt gradually—it will be a thick batter.

6. Cover and set in a warm place to rise for 45 minutes to 1 hour. It should approximately double in size.

7. Once the batter is ready, heat a large nonstick frying pan or griddle over medium heat. Have the lid ready nearby.

8. Generously grease the insides of 4 English muffin rings with butter or nonstick spray and place them in the pan.

9. Give the batter a gentle stir to break up the bubbles a bit, then spoon some batter into each ring. For 3½-inch rings, use a bit less than half a cup of batter—you may need to adjust if your rings are a different size.

10. Turn the heat down to medium-low.

11. Put the lid on the pan and let cook for 5 minutes, or until the muffins are golden brown on the bottom. You should see bubbles rising up, and the top of the muffin should be set, not liquid.

12. Pull off the rings if they'll come easily (if not, leave them on), and flip the muffins over.

13. Put the lid back on and cook for another 3 to 5 minutes, until browned on the other side.

14. Turn the heat back up to medium, re-grease the rings, and repeat with the remaining batter.

15. Let the muffins cool a bit, then split them carefully with a fork. Serve with jam and butter or clotted cream.

Friendly Advice: These freeze well and are so much better than store-bought that it's worth making a big batch. When you cut them in half, use a fork to split them apart rather than a knife—it maximizes the "nooks and crannies" that crisp up when you toast them.

Comforting Gruel

Mrs. March gave the mother tea and gruel, and comforted her with promises of help, while she dressed the little baby as tenderly as if it had been her own.

CHAPTER 2: "A MERRY CHRISTMAS"

From the way gruel is often described in fiction, as something freezing peasants or jailed criminals have to survive on, we expected this to be terrible. However, it's actually very tasty, like a thinner, drinkable oatmeal. Perfect for a breakfast on the go, or for someone in bed with a cold.

Makes 1 serving

- ¼ cup rolled oats
- 2⅓ cups cold water, divided
- small handful of raisins (optional)
- ¼ teaspoon salt
- 2 teaspoons brown sugar
- ⅛ teaspoon freshly grated nutmeg

1. Grind the rolled oats in a food processor until they're about the consistency of coarse cornmeal.

2. Mix the ground oats with ⅓ cup cold water in a small bowl or mug and stir well. Set aside.

3. Bring the remaining 2 cups water to a boil in a medium skillet.

4. Add the soaked oatmeal and stir well. Add a handful of raisins if desired and let it all boil over medium heat for 8 to 10 minutes, until thickened but still liquid. Keep stirring to keep it from clumping.

5. Transfer the gruel back to the small bowl or mug. Add the salt, brown sugar, and nutmeg (adjust flavors as you like) and serve.

The Marches' "Merrycle" Christmas Dinner

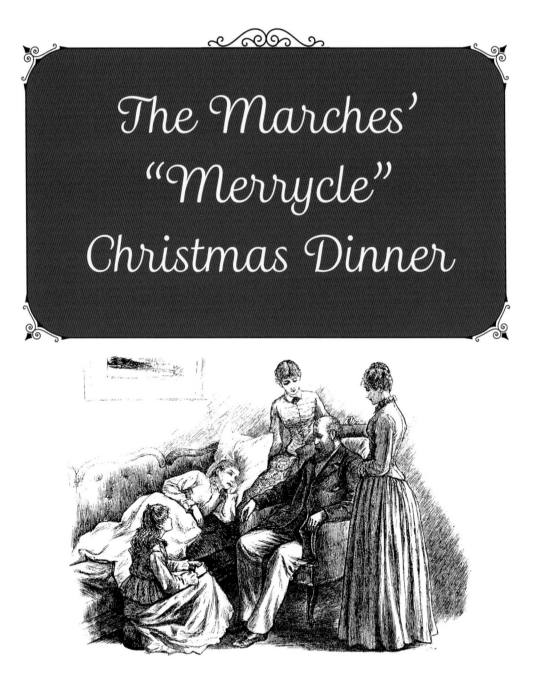

There never *was* such a Christmas dinner as they had that day. The fat turkey was a sight to behold, when Hannah sent him up, stuffed, browned, and decorated; so was the plum-pudding, which melted in one's mouth; likewise the jellies, in which Amy revelled like a fly in a honey-pot. Everything turned out well, which was a mercy, Hannah said, "For my mind was that flustered, mum, that it's a merrycle I didn't roast the pudding, and stuff the turkey with raisins, let alone bilin' of it in a cloth."

Mr. Laurence and his grandson dined with them, also Mr. Brooke,—at whom Jo glowered darkly, to Laurie's infinite amusement. Two easy-chairs stood side by side at the head of the table, in which sat Beth and her father, feasting modestly on chicken and a little fruit. They drank healths, told stories, sung songs, "reminisced," as the old folks say, and had a thoroughly good time. A sleigh-ride had been planned, but the girls would not leave their father; so the guests departed early, and, as twilight gathered, the happy family sat together round the fire.

CHAPTER 22: "PLEASANT MEADOWS"

Just one year after the "Christmas without any presents" at the beginning of the book, Mr. March returns from the war after a long illness. Mrs. March had gone away to Washington to nurse him, and Beth nearly died from scarlet fever during her absence, so having everyone home together and alive is a huge relief.

It turns out Father has returned just in time for Christmas dinner, and it's merry indeed, with a very traditional menu of roast turkey, plum-pudding, and cranberry jelly. For sides, we'd recommend Beth's "The History of a Squash" (page 70), Mrs. Kirke's stewed onions (page 60), and Hannah's cale-cannon (page 138).

Turkey a Sight to Behold

Just like Christmas without presents, turkey isn't turkey without gravy!
Serve with ham or tongue (page 90), and cranberry jelly (page 159).

- ¾ cup (1½ sticks) butter plus ½ cup (1 stick) softened butter, divided
- 2 cups chopped ham, about 9 ounces
- 1 fresh turkey, including the giblets, 12 to 14 pounds
- 6 cups fresh bread crumbs, about 11 ounces
- ⅛ teaspoon freshly grated nutmeg
- 2 tablespoons chopped fresh marjoram leaves
- 1½ teaspoons grated lemon zest
- 1 teaspoon lemon juice
- ½ teaspoon pepper, plus more for seasoning
- 4 egg yolks, beaten
- 2½ tablespoons salt, divided, plus more for seasoning
- ¾ cup flour, divided
- 3 cups water

1. Melt ¾ cup of the butter in a small saucepan over medium heat and set aside.

2. Pulse the ham in a food processor until it's finely minced.

3. Take the giblets and neck out of the turkey's cavity. Wash the turkey in cold water, rinsing out the cavity, and pat dry.

4. Preheat the oven to 500°F.

5. In a large bowl, mix the bread crumbs and minced ham together. Add the nutmeg, marjoram, lemon zest, lemon juice, and ½ teaspoon pepper, and mix.

6. Mix in the ½ cup softened butter. Add in the beaten yolks. (It's easiest to mix with your hands at this point.) Set the stuffing aside.

7. Rub ½ tablespoon salt and plenty of pepper into the walls of the turkey's cavity.

8. Dredge the outside of the turkey with ½ cup of the flour, or more if needed. Shake off the excess.

9. Place the turkey in a roasting pan, breast-side up. Brush with the melted butter and sprinkle with 1 tablespoon of the salt and plenty of pepper. Turn the

bird over so it's breast-side down, then baste with melted butter, and sprinkle with 1 more tablespoon of salt and lots of pepper.

10. Fluff the stuffing with your hand and pack it loosely into the turkey's cavity.

11. Tie the legs together securely with cooking twine, so the bird keeps its shape and the stuffing doesn't fall out.

12. Roast for 15 minutes.

13. Start the giblet stock for the gravy: put the giblets and water in a medium pot over high heat and bring to a boil, skimming the scum frequently. Lower to a steady simmer for 1½ hours. Strain and discard the giblets (unless your family loves liver—if they do, you can mash a bit of it into your gravy).

14. After the first 15 minutes of cooking, take the turkey out of the oven and lower the temperature to 325°F.

15. Baste the turkey with melted butter before putting it back in the oven, and baste again every 30 minutes thereafter. Start checking the internal temperature a full hour before you expect the turkey to be done; a good rule of thumb is to allow 15 to 20 minutes per pound. Take the turkey out of the oven when the internal temperature of the breast hits 155°F and the thigh hits 165°F.

16. Take the turkey out of the oven, lift the bird out onto a baking sheet, cover the top with foil, and let it rest for 20 minutes.

17. Take the drippings and put them in a deep skillet over medium-high heat until bubbling.

18. In a small bowl, add a small ladleful of the giblet stock to the remaining ¼ cup flour and whisk together till smooth. Add it to the drippings and whisk over the medium-high heat until the whole mixture is bubbling—it should take just a few minutes. Mash a bit of the liver into it if desired. Add giblet stock and whisk together, and once it bubbles again after a few minutes, the gravy is done.

19. Remove and discard the string tying the legs together. Take out the stuffing from the cavity with a wooden spoon, and serve it in a bowl.

Friendly Advice: If flavor is more important to you than aesthetics, or you're going to carve up the turkey before sending it out to the table anyway, try roasting the turkey breast-side down, as this recipe directs—the lean white meat will cook in the juices and keep from drying out.

Melt-in-One's-Mouth Plum-Pudding

This is a half-recipe of a classic plum-pudding. We're not talking about chocolate pudding cups (as many Americans might think when they hear "pudding"). The March family would be more familiar with the boiled or steamed kind of pudding, which is more like a dense cake or bread-pudding in texture, and still a favorite dessert in British cuisine.

This is a two-day project requiring some unusual kitchen equipment! You'll need a pudding cloth (a 20 x 20-inch square of unbleached cotton muslin), tongs, rubber gloves, a clean flat surface, a flat-bottom cup or glass, and large pot that is at least 7 inches tall (but the deeper, the better) with a fitted lid. You have to be able to submerge the pudding easily without it touching the bottom, but note that the water will also boil over and spill if the pot isn't deep enough and you don't put enough space between the surface of the water and the top of the pot. Suet can also be difficult to find, especially in the U.S. Check with a local butcher—you'd be looking for beef kidney suet, and you'll have to pick the fat from the membranes and mince it with a knife or food processor. (If you don't want to go to the trouble, or if you're vegetarian, you can just use more butter.)

Makes 6 to 8 servings

- 2 cups milk
- ½ pound white bread, including the crusts, torn or cut into small chunks
- ¼ cup plus ½ tablespoon flour, divided
- 6 tablespoons sugar
- ½ teaspoon freshly grated nutmeg
- ½ teaspoon ground cinnamon
- ¼ teaspoon ground cloves

- 3 eggs, beaten
- 2 tablespoons butter
- 2 tablespoons minced suet (or more butter, finely diced)
- ¼ to ½ pound raisins, depending on how much you like raisins
- pudding sauce, for serving (see recipe on page 158)

NIGHT BEFORE:

1. If your pudding cloth is new, wash it using unscented detergent; dry it; and set it aside for the next day.

2. Scald the milk: Pour milk into a medium heavy saucepan. Slowly warm over medium heat, stirring often to keep the milk from thickening or burning. Once it's steamy and bubbles start appearing at the edge, remove from the heat.

3. In a medium heatproof bowl, pour the milk onto the bread, mix briefly, cover, and let soak overnight in the refrigerator.

AT LEAST FOUR HOURS BEFORE DINNER:

1. Whisk together ½ tablespoon of the flour with the sugar, nutmeg, cinnamon, and cloves.

2. In a large bowl, mix the dry ingredients with the soaked bread, eggs, butter, and suet. (If you don't have suet, you can use more butter, finely diced.) Stir thoroughly.

3. Mix in the raisins to taste. If you absolutely adore raisins, use ½ pound. Otherwise, ¼ pound is probably plenty.

4. Soak the pudding cloth in plenty of cold water in your largest, deepest pot, and bring it to a boil over high heat. If it's the first time you're using the cloth, boil for 20 minutes. (After the first time, you will only need to boil it for 5 minutes.)

5. Pull out the pudding cloth using tongs, and wearing thick rubber dishwashing gloves, wring out the excess water. Hold the cloth to the light and make sure there are no holes. (If there are holes where you will put the pudding batter, it won't work!)

6. Spread the cloth flat on a clean surface.

7. Discard the old water and fill your large pot again as full as possible, while leaving space at the top so it doesn't boil over. Put a small plate upside down at the bottom of the pot—this keeps the wrapped pudding from hitting the bottom of the pot and burning. Turn the heat to high and cover with a lid.

8. While you're waiting for the water to boil, spread the remaining ¼ cup flour over the cloth and rub it into the wet fabric with your hand or a flat-bottomed cup or glass. Use more flour if needed. You should pull out the creases so you don't end up with any spots you haven't floured. You know the cloth is ready when you've rubbed enough flour

The March Family

into it to have dry flour on top of the fabric. Shake off the extra flour.

9. Put the pudding batter in the middle of the cloth.

10. Gather up all the corners of the cloth and sides, so they're all in your hand and there are no open gaps. Tie cooking twine as close to the pudding as you can. Use plenty of twine because you'll need to go around and around—wrap the twine around, pull tight, and repeat. Tie the ends of the twine into loops.

11. Wait until the water comes to a rolling boil over high heat.

12. Drop the pudding into the pot, making sure it's fully submerged. Cover and boil for 2½ to 3 hours. It's important that there be plenty of water that's boiling the whole time. If you need to add water, make sure it's boiling hot—don't add cold water.

13. Have ready a large bowl full of cold water. When the pudding is finished boiling, plunge it into the cold water briefly. Hang it up to drip-dry till you're ready to serve.

14. Cut or untie the twine to open the bag, and turn the pudding over onto a plate.

15. Cut into slices and eat with pudding sauce.

Plum–Pudding Sauce

- 3 tablespoons packed brown sugar
- 1½ tablespoons butter
- 1 tablespoon flour
- ½ cup boiling water
- a few drops of lemon juice

1. Combine the brown sugar, butter, and flour in a small saucepan. Stir together until lighter in color.

2. Add the boiling water and stir until the butter is melted and the sugar is dissolved.

3. Cook over medium-high heat until the sauce boils.

4. Stir in the lemon juice.

Cranberry Jelly

This makes a beautiful clear jelly with a deep ruby color. A jelly bag is nice to have for this—it's a muslin bag that hangs on a stand over a bowl, allowing the juice to drain out slowly without any pulp getting through. You can rig up a makeshift version by lining a colander with several layers of cheesecloth and setting it over a bowl.

Makes about 1 cup

- 10 ounces fresh or frozen cranberries
- 1 cup sugar

1. Boil the cranberries in enough water to cover them, until the berries have all burst and are very soft.

2. Get a jelly bag wet and wring it out. Set it up on the stand over a bowl.

3. Pour the cranberries into the bag and let the juice drain out into the bowl overnight. Do not squeeze it out or the jelly will be cloudy.

4. Discard the cranberry pulp.

5. Put a small plate in the freezer, and put the juice and sugar in a small saucepan.

6. Bring to a strong boil, with lots of bubbles all over the surface (but don't let it boil over). Skim off any foam.

7. Reduce the heat to low and boil for 5 to 10 minutes, stirring often, until you can see it starting to thicken a bit when you let it run off the spoon, or until it reaches 220°F on a candy thermometer (an instant-read or laser thermometer doesn't work well for this).

8. Test it by dropping a small spoonful on the cold plate and putting it back in the freezer for 1 minute. Take it out again and push your finger through the jelly on the plate. If it wrinkles as you push it, it's done. If not, keep boiling and try again in a few minutes.

9. Once done, transfer the jelly to a jar through a fine strainer and process it for canning if you like, or just store it in the refrigerator—it will last up to three months.

Happy Surprise Tea

Mercy on us, how they did talk! first one, then the other, then all burst out together, trying to tell the history of three years in half an hour. It was fortunate that tea was at hand, to produce a lull and provide refreshment, for they would have been hoarse and faint if they had gone on much longer. Such a happy procession as filed away into the little dining-room! Mr. March proudly escorted "Mrs. Laurence;" Mrs. March as proudly leaned on the arm of "my son;" the old gentleman took Jo, with a whispered "You must be my girl now," and a glance at the empty corner by the fire, that made Jo whisper back, with trembling lips, "I'll try to fill her place, sir."

The twins pranced behind, feeling that the millennium was at hand, for every one was so busy with the new-comers that they were left to revel at their own sweet will, and you may be sure they made the most of the opportunity. Didn't they steal sips of tea, stuff gingerbread *ad libitum*, get a hot biscuit apiece, and, as a crowning trespass, didn't they each whisk a captivating little tart into their tiny pockets, there to stick and crumble treacherously, teaching them that both human nature and pastry are frail?

CHAPTER 43: "SURPRISES"

It's Jo's birthday and she's wondering what she should do with her life when surprise! Amy and Laurie are back from Europe, and surprise! They got married! Jo is truly happy for them, but she's feeling a little lonely and left out until ... there's a knock at the front door and surprise! It's Professor Bhaer! She's so excited to see him that she clutches at his coat, takes his hat, and basically drags him inside to join the impromptu family party.

Hannah raids the pantry for snacks (one should always have emergency gingerbread handy) and whips up a quick batch of hot biscuits and tarts for tea. Everyone is quite interested to meet this professor they've heard so much about, and they all settle in for a happy celebration.

Hot Biscuits

Nowadays we expect quite a bit more butter in a biscuit, but Mrs. Cornelius calls for only "a piece of butter half the size of an egg"! Surprisingly, these still turn out light and fluffy, with a tangy buttermilk flavor almost like sourdough. Using self-rising flour is convenient because it already has the salt and baking powder measured for you. Baking soda and baking powder were fairly new at the time, in a slightly different form than we use now, but the basic composition of a biscuit has lasted 150 years.

Makes 7 (3-inch) biscuits

- 2 cups self-rising flour
- 2 tablespoons cold unsalted butter, cubed
- 1 cup buttermilk, plus a bit extra for brushing the tops
- butter, jam, or honey, for serving

1. Preheat the oven to 425°F.

2. Measure the flour into a large bowl.

3. Add the butter and cut it into the flour with a pastry blender or rub it in with your fingers. (You can also use a food processor if you're feeling newfangled.) The texture should look like coarse cornmeal.

4. Stir in the buttermilk until just combined, and turn the dough out onto a lightly floured board. The dough will start out crumbly and shaggy in a big messy pile, but don't worry! Just keep going and all will be well.

5. Scoot the edges of the dough into a vaguely rectangular shape, and pat it down to about 1 inch thick. Fold it in half, then pat down again to 1 inch thick. Put any stray flour bits on top.

6. Fold it in half again, in the opposite direction. Repeat once or twice more, until the dough is mostly holding together.

7. Pat out the dough to 1 inch thick, and cut out the biscuits with a 3-inch biscuit cutter or the floured rim of a glass. Make sure to cut straight down without twisting—this will help them rise while baking. Gather the scraps together and gently form them into your last biscuit or two.

8. Place the biscuits close together in a medium cast-iron pan or in a circle on a baking sheet, edges touching each other but not squashed in. Brush the tops with buttermilk.

9. Bake 15 minutes or until golden brown on top.

10. Serve hot with butter and jam or honey.

Friendly Advice: Seven biscuits allows for one in the center and six around it, which fits well in a medium cast-iron skillet.

The March Family

Gingerbread to Stuff Ad Libitum

Gingerbread is the most frequently recurring food in *Little Women*. This one is a dark, intense gingerbread with a strong molasses flavor—definitely more of a bread than a dessert.

Makes 1 (9 x 5-inch) loaf

- 2 tablespoons water
- 1 teaspoon baking soda
- ½ cup butter plus more for greasing
- ½ teaspoon salt
- 1 cup molasses
- 3 scant cups flour
- 1 tablespoon ground ginger
- ½ teaspoon ground cinnamon
- ½ teaspoon ground cloves
- ½ cup packed dark brown sugar
- 2 eggs
- 1 cup buttermilk

1. Preheat the oven to 350°F. Grease and flour a 9 x 5-inch loaf pan.

2. In a small pot, boil the water and add the baking soda. Let it foam up, and then let it sit for 5 minutes.

3. Add the butter and salt, then stir until it melts.

4. Whisk in the molasses. Let cool while you get the dry ingredients together.

5. In a large bowl, sift the flour, ginger, cinnamon, and cloves together, then whisk in the sugar.

6. In a medium bowl, whisk the eggs and buttermilk together, then add the molasses mixture and stir to combine.

7. Pour the wet ingredients into the dry ingredients and stir well.

8. Pour the batter into the prepared pan and bake for about 1 hour, until the bread just begins to pull away from the edge of the pan. A toothpick inserted in the center should come out clean.

9. Remove from oven and cool on a rack for 15 minutes before serving. This bread tastes best the next day.

Captivating Little Tarts

Just in case you ever happen to find yourself in this situation, these tarts are a good way to use up the various kinds of jelly you've made while testing recipes for a cookbook!

Makes about 15 tarts

- 1 Double Pie Crust (page 63)
- ½ cup jelly or jam, any kind you like
- 1 egg, beaten

1. Preheat the oven to 350°F.

2. Roll out the pie dough in a rectangular shape ¼ inch thick, and cut it into 3-inch squares.

3. Put about ½ tablespoon of jelly in the center of each square, and brush the edges with beaten egg.

4. Pick up the corners of each square and gather them in the center, pressing the edges together.

5. Transfer the tarts to a baking sheet, and brush the tops with more beaten egg.

6. Bake for 10 to 15 minutes, or until golden brown.

Friendly Advice: Be careful not to get overexcited and put too much jelly in—the tarts will overflow and be a pain to clean up.

Apple-Picking Holiday

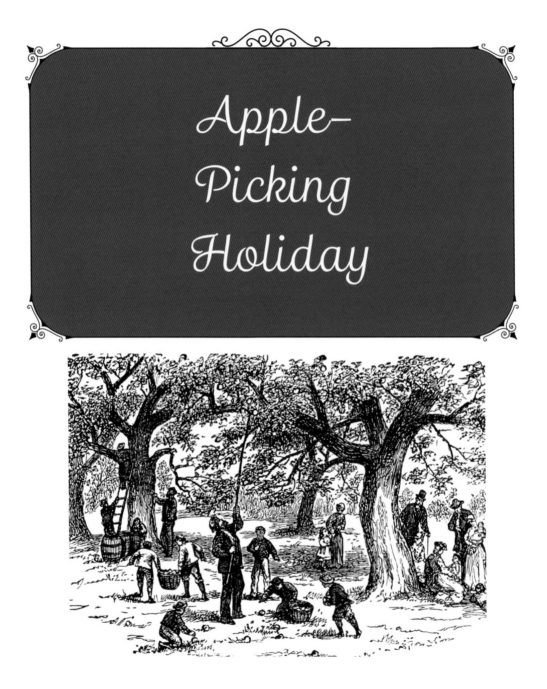

There were a great many holidays at Plumfield, and one of the most delightful was the yearly apple-picking; for then the Marches, Laurences, Brookes, and Bhaers turned out in full force and made a day of it. [...]

Then Jo and Meg, with a detachment of the bigger boys, set forth the supper on the grass, for an out-of-door tea was always the crowning joy of the day. The land literally flowed with milk and honey on such occasions, for the lads were not required to sit at table, but allowed to partake of refreshment as they liked,—freedom being the sauce best beloved by the boyish soul. They availed themselves of the rare privilege to the fullest extent, for some tried the pleasing experiment of drinking milk while standing on their heads, others lent a charm to leap-frog by eating pie in the pauses of the game, cookies were sown broadcast over the field, and apple turn-overs roosted in the trees like a new style of bird. The little girls had a private tea-party, and Ted roved among the edibles at his own sweet will.

Chapter 47: "Harvest Time"

Phew, we can all relax! We are at the novel's epilogue, which shows us that the Marches are living happily ever after. Nothing is perfect, of course. Beth's absence will forever be a hole in their hearts, and her namesake, Amy and Laurie's daughter, is sickly and might not live long. (Spoiler from the sequels: She does live and grows up to be lovely.) But despite their sadness, the sisters are at the center of a contented, joyful, flourishing family, and they have chosen paths full of love and fulfillment.

It's especially satisfying to see that Jo has found her purpose in the school she's started with Professor Bhaer. She's happy to have this huge project for all that restless energy she's had pent up all her life. By establishing and leading a house full of boys, she's also created a place for herself where she won't be as hampered by society's limited expectations for women. Not having to be ladylike all the time? What freedom that is for Jo!

The family remains as close as ever, starting new cozy traditions, like this annual harvest holiday to celebrate their crop of apples and kids. This year, they celebrate Marmee's 60th birthday with a glorious outdoor tea. And so, we close this cookbook as the novel does, with apple turn-overs (page 136), pie, cookies, and tea *al fresco*.

Charming Ham Pie for Leapfrog

A cold meat pie could be made ahead for a holiday and then readily cut into slices to carry around—no wonder it was such a popular choice for outdoor picnics. Not to mention, it looks impressive with lots of decorations on the crust and feeds a ton of people, so it's an excellent party dish.

Makes 1 (9-inch) pie

For the hot water crust:
- 6 tablespoons lard, diced
- 6 tablespoons butter, diced
- 1 scant cup water
- 5 cups flour
- 1½ teaspoons salt
- 2 beaten eggs plus another one for brushing the crust

For the pie filling:
- 3 tablespoons butter
- 1 pound white mushrooms, thinly sliced
- 1 small onion, diced
- 2 sprigs plus 1 teaspoon fresh thyme leaves, divided
- ¾ tablespoon plus a pinch of salt, divided
- pepper
- 2 pounds diced ham
- 2 tablespoons chopped fresh parsley, divided

- 1 teaspoon chopped fresh sage
- ¼ teaspoon ground allspice
- 3 large boneless chicken breasts, diced into ½-inch cubes
- ½ teaspoon ground mace
- zest of 1 lemon
- 6 eggs, hard-boiled, peeled, and left whole

For the jellied stock:
- 1 tablespoon powdered gelatin
- ¼ cup water
- 1 cup chicken stock
- mustard, for serving

PREPARE THE HOT WATER CRUST:

1. Put the lard, butter, and water in a medium saucepan and gently warm over low heat until melted; do not let it boil.

2. Stir together the flour and salt in a large bowl. Make a hollow in the center and add the two beaten eggs, stirring them gently around with a knife so they are half mixed with the flour.

3. Pour in the melted fat and water and mix together to form a soft dough; add up to 3 tablespoons extra warm water if it is too dry. Knead gently, adding more flour if it is too sticky to handle.

4. Wrap the dough in plastic wrap and refrigerate until cold, at least 1 hour.

PREPARE THE PIE FILLING:

1. Heat the butter in a medium skillet over medium-high heat.

2. Add the mushrooms and onion, and sauté with the sprigs of thyme, a pinch of salt, and lots of pepper.

3. In a large bowl, mix the cold ham with 1 tablespoon parsley and the sage, allspice, and pepper to taste. In another large bowl, mix the diced chicken with ¾ tablespoons salt, the remaining 1 tablespoon parsley, 1 teaspoon fresh thyme, and the mace, lemon zest, and pepper to taste.

ASSEMBLE AND BAKE THE PIE:

1. Preheat oven to 350°F. Grease a 9 x 3-inch round pan with a removable bottom with butter.

2. Cut off a generous quarter of the pastry and keep in the fridge, for the lid.

3. On a floured surface, roll out the rest of the pastry into a 13 to 14-inch circle, about ⅓-inch thick.

4. Use this to line the cake pan, pressing the pastry into the sides and flattening any overlap with your fingers. It should come 2½ to 3 inches up the sides of the pan.

5. Put half of the ham at the bottom of the pie, then the chicken, then the whole boiled eggs, the mushrooms and onions, and finally another layer of ham. Mound it up a little so that the top of the pie is convex rather than concave.

6. Roll out the reserved piece of pastry into a circle about the size of the pan. Brush the edges of the lining pastry with a little of the remaining beaten egg (you'll need the rest later), and lay the pastry lid on top of the pie. Crimp the edges so they are sealed inside the pan—don't crimp them onto the edge of the pan as you usually would for a pie, because doing so will keep you from removing it nicely from the pan.

7. Cut a 2-inch diameter hole in the center of the pastry lid. Make a coil rim with extra pastry around the edge of the hole. This will help keep the liquid inside from bubbling out as it cooks.

8. Decorate the top of the pie with extra pastry, as you choose—you can make leaves, flowers, stars, or letters.

9. Bake for 30 minutes. Reduce the temperature to 325°F and bake for 1 hour and 15 minutes more. If the top crust is concave instead of convex, a pool of juice and fat may form around the center hole during baking that you'll want to remove with a turkey baster, or the crust may become soggy.

10. Remove the pie from the oven and carefully release it from the pan.

11. Brush the top and sides of the pie with beaten egg and cook for another 15 minutes to set the glaze.

PREPARE THE JELLIED STOCK AND SERVE:

1. Take the pie out of the oven and allow to cool completely.

2. Meanwhile, put the powdered gelatin in the ¼ cup water and let it sit for 10 minutes. Whisk into the chicken stock.

3. Heat the stock in a small pan over low heat until it's just pourable—not too hot.

4. Pour the jellied stock slowly into the center hole in the pie. The filling will have shrunk, creating a space around the edge that is traditionally filled with jellied stock. Refrigerate to let the gelatin set.

5. Serve the pie cold or at room temperature, in slices with mustard.

Cookies to Eat in a Field

Simple sugar cookies, flavored with nutmeg. You could use pre-ground nutmeg for this, but freshly grated is recommended. These are very nice dipped in milk, as the Plumfield boys would have done for the outdoor harvest supper.

Makes 2 dozen (2½-inch) cookies

- 1¾ cups flour
- heaping ½ teaspoon baking soda
- ½ whole nutmeg, grated or 1½ teaspoons ground nutmeg
- ¼ cup white sugar
- ½ cup brown sugar
- ½ cup butter
- 1 large egg
- ¼ cup heavy cream

1. Mix the flour and baking soda together in a medium bowl. Grate the nutmeg into the bowl, and sift together. Set aside.

2. In a large bowl, beat the white sugar, brown sugar, and butter until light and fluffy.

3. In a small bowl, beat the egg and add the cream to it. Add the egg mixture gradually to the butter and sugar, then beat.

4. Gradually add the dry ingredients into the wet until well mixed. Add a little extra flour at a time if it's too sticky to handle, but the softer the dough, the better the cookie will be.

5. Wrap the dough and refrigerate for 2 hours until firm.

6. Preheat the oven to 375°F and line baking sheets with parchment paper.

7. Roll out the dough on a lightly floured surface till it's ½ inch thick.

8. Cut with a 2½-inch round cutter or a drinking glass. Line up on the baking sheets, at least 1 inch apart.

9. Bake for about 14 minutes or until lightly browned. Cool on baking sheets for 2 minutes. Remove to wire racks to cool completely.

The March Family

Party Tea

Louisa May Alcott's mother put this recipe for making tea in her little leather-covered book in 1856: "The proper way to make a cup of good tea, is a matter of some importance. The teapot is at once filled up with boiling water; then the tea is put into the pot, and is allowed to stand five minutes before it is used. The leaves gradually absorb the water, and as gradually sink to the bottom. The result is, that the tea leaves are not scalded, as they are when boiling water is poured over them, and you get all the true flavor of the tea. In truth, much less is required this way than under the old and common practice."[10]

10   Collins, *The Little Women Treasury*, 66.

Makes 4 servings

- 10 cups water
- 3 tablespoons loose tea leaves

1. Bring the water to a boil.

2. Pour 4 cups of boiling water into a large teapot, let it sit for 5 minutes, and then pour it out. (This step is called scalding the teapot.)

3. Pour another 4 cups boiling water into the teapot, and add tea leaves. Pour the remaining water into a smaller teapot so it's available for people who don't like strong tea to dilute their cup.

4. Let the tea steep—5 to 6 minutes for green tea, 10 to 12 for black tea—before pouring. (You can also try mixing half green and half black.)

Tidbit of History: Spilling the Tea

In 1773, anger over British taxes led to the Boston Tea Party, where demonstrators dumped 342 chests of tea into the harbor. During the American Revolution, it was considered unpatriotic to drink tea. After the war was over, America began trading directly with China (and later Japan), and tea slowly trickled back into the daily diet. By the 1860s, New York City boasted an impressive selection of tea shops. One of them, The Great American Tea Company, became the largest tea distributor in the country. (By the way, The Great American Tea Company eventually expanded its business, renamed itself A&P, and was the biggest grocery retailer in the U.S. for 60 years.)

The Great American Tea Company posted advertisements that listed their goods and prices in *Godey's Lady's Book*, one of the most popular 19th-century magazines. Some of their varieties are familiar to us, others not so much: For black teas, they offered Oolong and English Breakfast; for green, they had Imperial, Japan, Young Hyson, and the excitingly named Gunpowder.[11]

---

11   Louis A. Godey and Sarah J. Hale, *Godey's Lady's Book*, (Philadelphia: Louis A. Godey, 1867).

Further Reading

HISTORICAL COOKBOOKS CONSULTED

Our recipes were based on historical receipts from the following books:

Acton, Eliza. *Modern Cookery*. London: Longmans, Green, Reader, and Dyer, 1868.

Alcott, Abba May. *Abigail May Alcott's Receipts & Simple Remedies*. Concord, MA: Nancy L. Kohl and the Louisa May Alcott Foundation, 1980.

Beauvilliers, A. B. *The Art of French Cookery*. London: Longman, Rees, Orme, Brown, and Green, 1827.

Beeton, Isabella. *Mrs Beeton's Book of Household Management*. London: S. O. Beeton, 1861.

Brisse, Léon. *Le calendrier gastronomique*. Paris: Bureaux de la Liberté, 1867.

Cardelli, P. and J.-S. Lionnet-Clémandot. *Nouveau manuel complet du confiseur et du chocolatier*. Paris: Librairie encyclopédique de Roret, 1862.

Carême, Marie-Antoine. *The Royal Parisian Pastrycook and Confectioner*. London: F. J. Mason, 1834.

Child, Lydia Maria. *The American Frugal Housewife*. Boston: Carter, Hendee, & Co., 1832.

Cornelius, Mary Hooker. *The Young Housekeeper's Friend*. Boston: Brown, Taggard, and Chase, 1859.

Dubois, Urbain. *Cuisine artistique: études de l'école moderne*. Paris: E. Dentu, 1872.

Dubois, Urbain, and Émile Bernard. *La cuisine classique*. Paris: E. Dentu, 1882.

Francatelli, Charles Elmé. *The Modern Cook*. London: Richard Bentley, 1846.

Francatelli, Charles Elmé. *The Royal English and Foreign Confectioner*. London: Chapman and Hall, 1862.

Hale, S. J. *The Good Housekeeper*. Boston: Weeks, Jordan, and Company, 1839.

Hall, Elizabeth M. *Practical American Cookery and Domestic Economy*. New York: C. M. Saxton, Barker & Co., 1860.

Knight S. G. *Tit-Bits: Or, How to Prepare a Nice Dish at a Moderate Expense*. Boston: Crosby and Nichols, 1864.

Leslie, Eliza. *Directions for Cookery, In Its Various Branches*. Philadelphia: Carey & Hart, 1840.

Leslie, Eliza. *Miss Leslie's Lady's New Receipt-Book*. Philadelphia: Carey & Hart, 1850.

Leslie, Eliza. *Seventy-Five Receipts for Pastry, Cakes, and Sweetmeats*. Boston: Munroe and Francis, 1828.

Viard, A. *Le cuisinier royal*. Paris: Gustave Barba, 1840.

Webster, A. L. *The Improved Housewife*. Boston: Phillips, Samson, and Company, 1855.

What Shall We Eat? A Manual for Housekeepers. New York: G. P. Putnam & Son, 1868.

WORKS CITED

If you'd like to know more fascinating historical details about Louisa May Alcott and life in 19th-century America, check out these sources:

Alcott, Louisa May. *Little Women: or, Meg, Jo, Beth, and Amy*. Boston: Little, Brown, and Company, 1896.

Collins, Carolyn Strom, and Christina Wyss Eriksson. *Little Women Treasury*. New York: Viking Penguin, 1996.

Gamber, Wendy. *The Boardinghouse in Nineteenth-Century America*. Baltimore: Johns Hopkins University Press, 2007.

Godey, Louis A., and Sarah J. Hale. *Godey's Lady's Book*. Philadelphia: Louis A. Godey, 1867.

Veit, Helen Zoe. *Food in the Civil War Era: The North*. East Lansing: Michigan State University Press, 2014.

OUR BLOG

Visit our blog, 36eggs.com, for extra recipes, more background information, and our detailed timeline of the *Little Women* novel, as well as lists of all the food and beverages that are mentioned in the story!

Further Reading

Acknowledgments

As librarians, we are obviously big fans of books, but we never expected to write one ourselves. And because we're newbie authors, it took the support of a whole village of friends, family, and kind strangers to complete this project, which is very dear to our hearts.

First, we would be remiss if we didn't thank our editor and publisher, Casie Vogel and Ulysses Press, for entrusting this book to us—it has been a great honor as well as a joy to work on. We are grateful too, to Lilly Ghahremani, our literary agent, for her invaluable guidance.

We would like to recognize the librarians, historians, and researchers who generously responded with enthusiasm and expertise when we contacted them out of the blue for advice: Michael Krondl, Helen Zoe Veit, Leslie Wilson, Erica J. Peters, Megan Elias, Valérie Dugas, Valérie Ammirati, Véronique Jira, and Loïc Bienassis.

We are also very grateful to our friends who helped us with the writing process. Their assistance included but was not limited to: searching for resources; editing, testing, and tasting recipes (even the weird ones); consulting as fellow fans of the novel, trying the many iterations of the personality quiz; and translating messages and information between English and French. Thank you to Beston Barnett, Erik Bergstrom, Vicki Bergstrom, Haley Bochler, Sara Coney, Susan Del Castillo, Molly Fischer, Jenn Frolich, Janet Gastil, Sarah Hiller-Venegas, Michael Ho, Hildie Kraus, Jennifer Lawson, Katherine Matlack, Matt Meola, Hannah O'Neill, Chisato Osada, Sarah Parylak, Lessa Pelayo-Lozada, Erin Pitts, Ramona Price, Phil Shopoff, Laurie Stein, Liz Vagani, Howie Wang, Alli Wilson, Nick Wilson, Laura Yamaguchi, and especially Whitney McBride-Carlson and Jamie Wilger.

About the Authors

JENNE BERGSTROM was raised by two summer camp directors but spent all her time reading instead of being outdoors. She went to a tiny one-room schoolhouse in a charming mountain town, but always dreamed of living in a glamorous big city. Nowadays, she lives in a tiny house in San Diego, and runs a library in another charming mountain town. She is the cofounder of the literary culinary blog 36eggs.com, and her favorite *Little Women* character is Aunt March.

MIKO OSADA is a librarian for kids and teens, in a suburb just east of San Diego. She lives with her wife and three cats, Figgy, Piggy, and Squeazle. Miko is the cocreator of 36eggs.com, a blog about re-creating fictitious dishes. *Little Women* was one of her favorite stories growing up, and she owns four copies of the book: two in Japanese (her first language) and two in English. Miko is a proud member of Slytherin House, and the March sister she relates to most is Amy.